Cartier's *La Grande Hermine*

for Roberta Briggs Kerr

The *Royal George*, an English man o' war of about 1760

A HISTORICAL ATLAS

EDITOR   D. G. G. Kerr, Professor of History at the University of Western Ontario

CARTOGRAPHY   preparation by Major C. C. J. Bond, D.L.S.
drawing by Ellsworth M. Walsh assisted by Edward Banks and Roy Petticrew

PUBLISHER   Thomas Nelson & Sons (Canada) Limited, 91 Wellington Street West, Toronto

OF CANADA

CREDITS

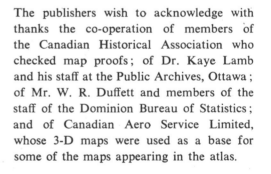

The publishers wish to acknowledge with thanks the co-operation of members of the Canadian Historical Association who checked map proofs; of Dr. Kaye Lamb and his staff at the Public Archives, Ottawa; of Mr. W. R. Duffett and members of the staff of the Dominion Bureau of Statistics; and of Canadian Aero Service Limited, whose 3-D maps were used as a base for some of the maps appearing in the atlas.

Map 3 is from Leverett and Taylor, in Atwood's *Physiographic Provinces of North America* (Ginn and Company, Toronto).

The ships shown in the preliminary pages and other drawings are by Mr. Roy Petticrew, who also redrew the old maps to a smaller scale and in a somewhat simplified form.

The *Halifax*, a blue-nose schooner built in Nova Scotia

FOREWORD

CONTENTS

The need for an adequate historical atlas of Canada has been strongly felt since the Second World War. The only existing atlas, that by the late Lawrence J. Burpee, was published in 1927. This pioneer work had long been out of print, and the passage of time and the progress of research had left it much in need of revision. In 1952, as President of the Canadian Historical Association, I discussed the problem with members of the Association and with Thomas Nelson & Sons (Canada) Limited, the publishers of the Burpee atlas; and the Council of the Association authorized the formation of a Committee to deal with the matter.

After further consideration, the Committee in 1954 recommended Professor D. G. G. Kerr to the publishers as an editor for a new atlas. From that time Professor Kerr carried the main weight of the project and took full responsibility for planning it. The Association's Committee has worked in a merely auxiliary capacity, advising the editor and the publishers as requested, and commenting on drafts of the maps and text. The editor became convinced at an early stage that to produce a mere revised version of Burpee's atlas, as had been considered, was neither practicable nor desirable under present-day conditions. All concerned agreed; and the volume now presented is an entirely new book conceived and executed by Mr. Kerr on quite different lines.

Careful consideration was given to the possibility of making the atlas bilingual. There were many objections to attempting to produce the text, and the nomenclature on maps, in both French and English within one set of covers; and it was generally agreed that a far more satisfactory solution would be the production of quite separate editions in the two languages. It is hoped, accordingly, that means can be found of publishing a French edition of the atlas at an early date.

Producing this completely original atlas has been a demanding task. On behalf of the Committee of the Canadian Historical Association which has followed the work, I should like to thank and congratulate Mr. Kerr, Thomas Nelson & Sons (Canada) Limited, and the various technical experts who have taken part. I hope and believe that all people who are interested in Canadian history, and particularly those who are teaching or studying the subject in schools or universities, will find the book valuable.

C. P. Stacey
Chairman
The Canadian Historical Association's
Committee on a Historical Atlas of Canada

CONTENTS

CONTINUED

CONTENTS
CONTINUED

EDITOR'S PREFACE

Canadian history includes much that can be fully understood only in relation to its geographical environment. This is true in particular of such topics as the explorations, the spread of settlement, the development of trade and transportation routes, the drawing of boundary lines, and the waging of wars. These, and much else in Canada's background, can hardly be studied therefore without a historical atlas of Canada and there has been none since L. J. Burpee's went out of print. The present volume, it is hoped, will remedy this deficiency.

In preparing it modern principles of map-making have been followed. Emphasis has been placed on simplicity and clarity with the elimination of unnecessary and cluttering detail. Physical features including relief have been shown on most maps and in as pictorial a fashion as possible. Names have been printed in readable dimensions. Certain additional features, however, that are not usual in historical atlases have been introduced. Maps all face the same way on the page and the text is always visible alongside the map it explains instead of being in some remote section by itself—innovations intended to make the volume easier to handle and use. Statistical diagrams and political charts are included, notably in a final section of the volume which summarizes developments since Confederation. Drawings from time to time decorate pages and serve also to show what early ships, fortifications, and so on, actually looked like. Colour has been used not only to enliven and help clarify maps and diagrams but also to differentiate from one another the main sections into which the atlas has been divided.

The problems of editing a historical atlas can be fully appreciated only by someone who has done so and then they will remain deeply ingrained in memory, frustrating and apparently infinite. Many are tedious and technical, ranging from the avoidance of inconsistencies and the endless checking of spelling and locations to decisions as to which details must be included and which others, imperceptibly less important, must be abandoned to avoid clutter. Some problems are more fundamental: to what extent should contemporary maps be reproduced; what emphasis should be placed on military or social or economic or political history; how should space be allocated as between recent and earlier periods; is it desirable in a reference work of this sort to be at all conclusive with regard to controversies such as those surrounding the Vikings and Cabot? In the midst of such problems and uncertainties, two things alone are clearly evident:

errors will not be entirely avoided and no reader will approve entirely the editor's judgement.

Nevertheless, the editing of this particular atlas was in many ways a most stimulating and rewarding experience. It involved the satisfying necessity of reviewing and re-thinking Canadian history in a comprehensive fashion while at the same time exploring certain quite important topics about which information in the usual secondary sources was scanty or inexact. Moreover, all was undertaken in company with a particularly gifted and congenial team of fellow workers, adding immeasurably to the value and pleasure of the experience. Grateful and sincere acknowledgements are made elsewhere of the assistance received from many sources but special mention must be made here of how much is owing to Colonel C. P. Stacey for his sound advice and meticulous attention to detail, to Major C. C. J. Bond for his expert knowledge of Canadian historical cartography and his hard work, and to Mr. R. I. K. Davidson for his artistic and imaginative designing of the individual pages and of the volume as a whole and for his special contributions in connection with the final statistical section.

D. G. G. Kerr

November, 1959.

The *Empress of Asia* sailing from Vancouver about 1905

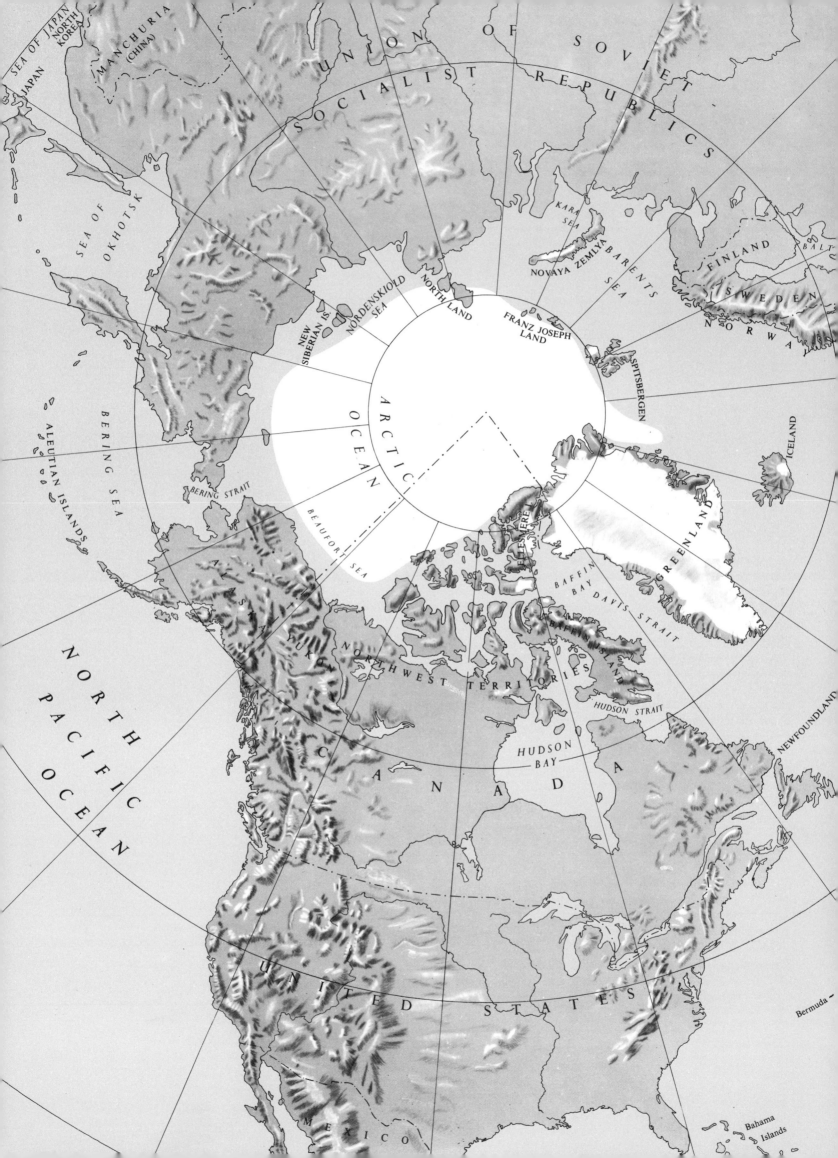

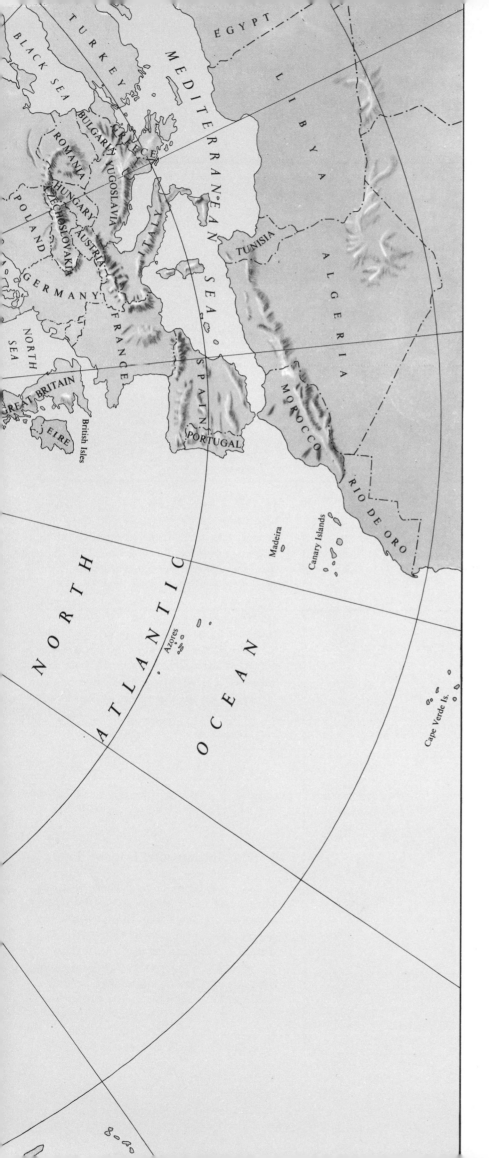

PART ONE

ENVIRONMENT AND

PREHISTORY

1 Canada and her Environment

Canada lay undiscovered, beyond the bounds of the known world, until recent centuries. Her history gradually began as she became part of a North Atlantic community centred in western Europe, a community to which Canada supplied fish and furs and later other products of her forests, fields, and mountains. The North Atlantic remained an area of vital importance to Canada even in the nineteenth century and afterwards, when transcontinental expansion made her more solidly North American and gave her an outlook on the Pacific as well. Most recently, a tilting world perspective has revealed a new neighbour across the North Pole.

2 The Ice Ages

The North American continent was gradually formed during millions of years by great upheavals and other changes in the earth's crust. In the most recent or Pleistocene geologic age (less than twenty million years

3 The Retreating Ice

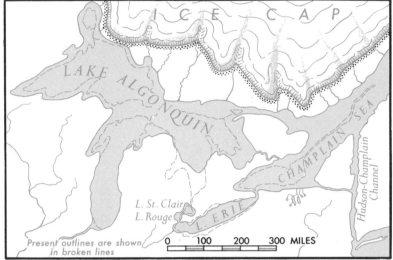

Present outlines are shown in broken lines

0 100 200 300 MILES

ago) there were successive Ice Ages during which huge glaciers carried with them into what is now the United States much of the surface of the Canadian Shield. At the same time they gouged out large troughs which, some thirty thousand years ago when the ice finally melted, became lakes and rivers—the canoe highways of the early explorers and traders. Later Canadian history, including for example the location of the Great Lakes and St. Lawrence section of the boundary with the United States, was also largely influenced by the movement of Pleistocene ice.

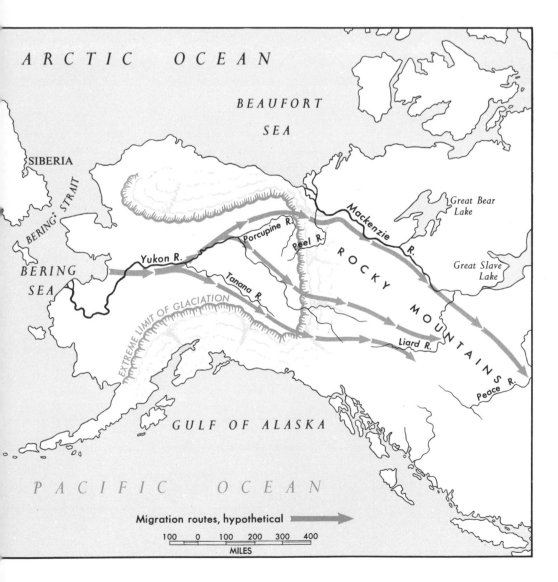

Migration routes, hypothetical ⟶

100 0 100 200 300 400
MILES

4 The Indian and Eskimo Entry

It has long been thought likely that the Indians and Eskimos entered North America by the easy passage from Siberia across the Bering Strait at the time when the retreating ice left a way open on the eastern slope of the Rockies between the Cordilleran and Keewatin Ice Caps. Archaeological investigation, still in its early stages, has strengthened this belief by the discovery of primitive stone implements and other remains at several points along probable routes.

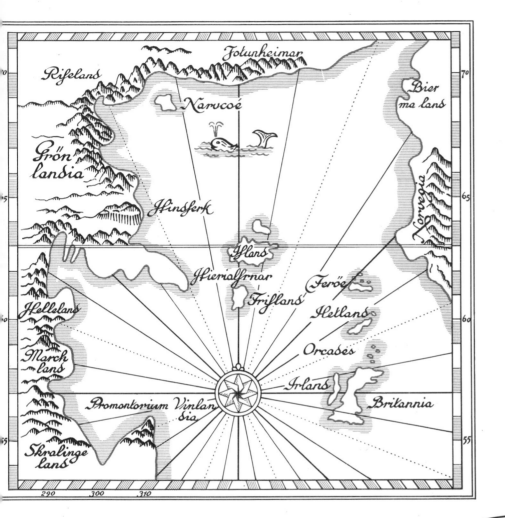

5 The Vikings in North America

References in Norse sagas show that the Vikings reached North America in the tenth or eleventh century. Their discoveries, almost unknown to the rest of Europe, seem to have had little or no influence on subsequent European or American history. Much controversy has resulted from attempts to locate such regions as Markland and Vinland, and from claims regarding the discovery of supposedly Viking relics at various places in North America. In fact, however, our certain knowledge of the Vikings in America is little clearer than that of the Icelander, Sigurdus Stephanius, whose map of 1570 is reproduced here.

6 The World of Martin Behaim, 1492

Behaim, a young German who had spent some time in Portugal, constructed in Nuremberg in 1492 a terrestrial globe. Its western hemisphere, shown here, makes clear that, although his view of the world was less accurate than that of the best geographers of his time, it was very similar to that on which Columbus based his journey westward that same year. There is no evidence that the two men may have met.

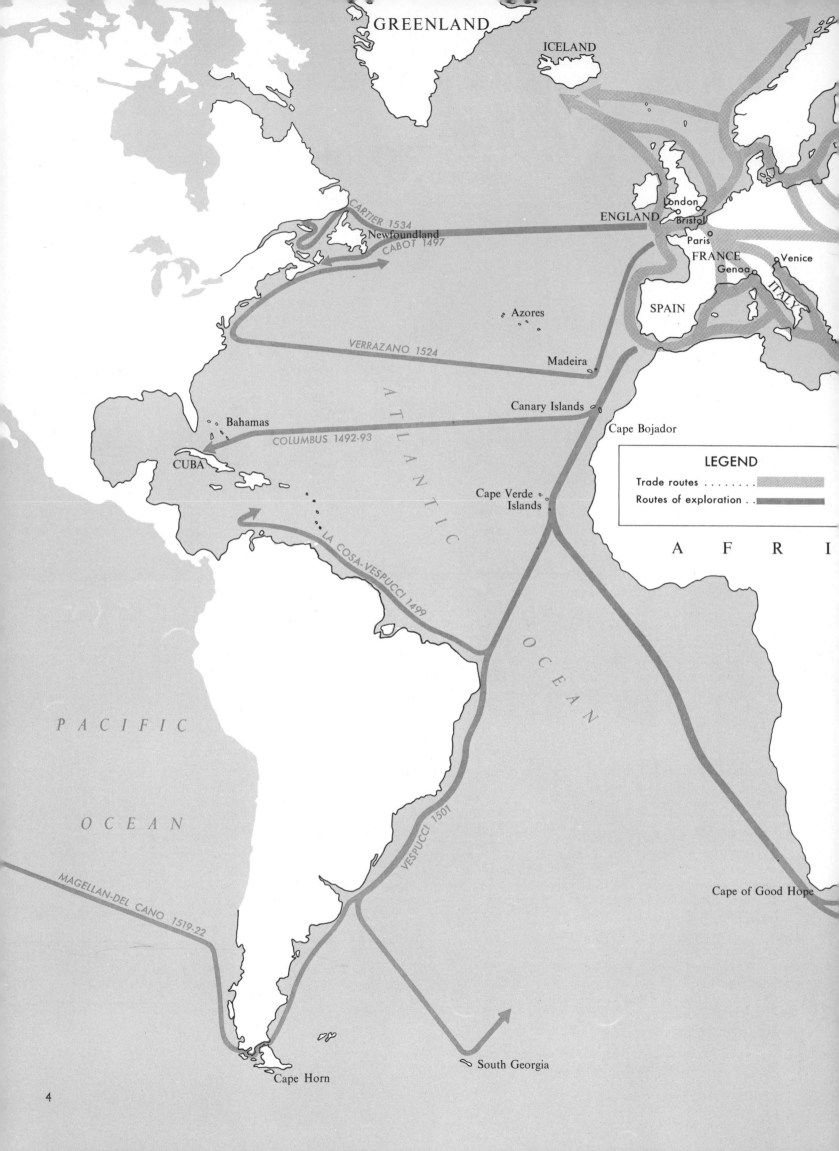

GREENLAND

ICELAND

CARTIER 1534

Newfoundland

CABOT 1497

ENGLAND

London

Bristol

Paris

FRANCE

Venice

Genoa

ITALY

Azores

SPAIN

Madeira

A T L A N T I C

Canary Islands

Cape Bojador

Bahamas

COLUMBUS 1492-93

CUBA

Cape Verde
Islands

VERRAZANO 1524

A F R I

LEGEND

Trade routes . . . .

Routes of exploration . .

LA COSA-VESPUCCI 1499

O C E A N

PACIFIC

OCEAN

VESPUCCI 1501

MAGELLAN-DEL CANO 1519-22

Cape of Good Hope

South Georgia

Cape Horn

4

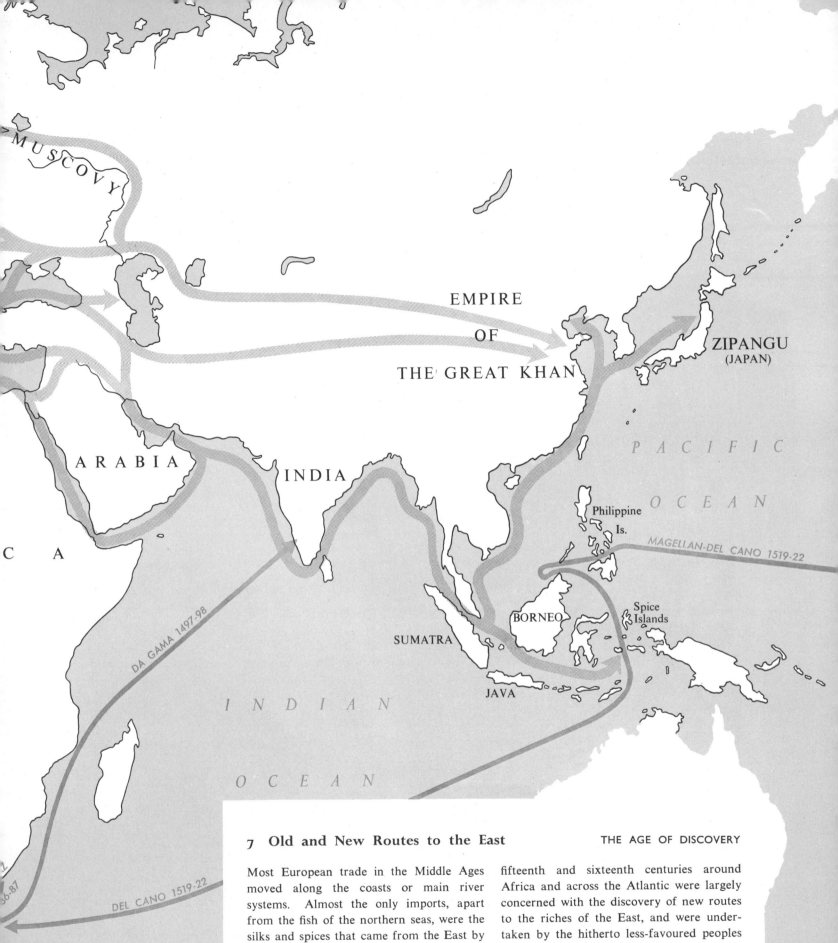

MUSCOVY

EMPIRE

OF

THE GREAT KHAN

ZIPANGU
(JAPAN)

ARABIA

INDIA

PACIFIC

OCEAN

Philippine
Is.

MAGELLAN-DEL CANO 1519-22

C A

DA GAMA 1497-98

BORNEO

Spice
Islands

SUMATRA

JAVA

I N D I A N

OCEAN

6-87

DEL CANO 1519-22

7 Old and New Routes to the East

Most European trade in the Middle Ages moved along the coasts or main river systems. Almost the only imports, apart from the fish of the northern seas, were the silks and spices that came from the East by caravan across Asia or by ship through the Persian Gulf or Red Sea. Italian seamen, especially the Venetians and the Genoese, dominated the principal trading area, the Mediterranean. The explorations of the fifteenth and sixteenth centuries around Africa and across the Atlantic were largely concerned with the discovery of new routes to the riches of the East, and were undertaken by the hitherto less-favoured peoples of Western Europe, the Portuguese, Spanish, English, French, and Dutch. At first, however, all but the Portuguese had frequently to employ experienced Italian seamen such as Columbus and Cabot.

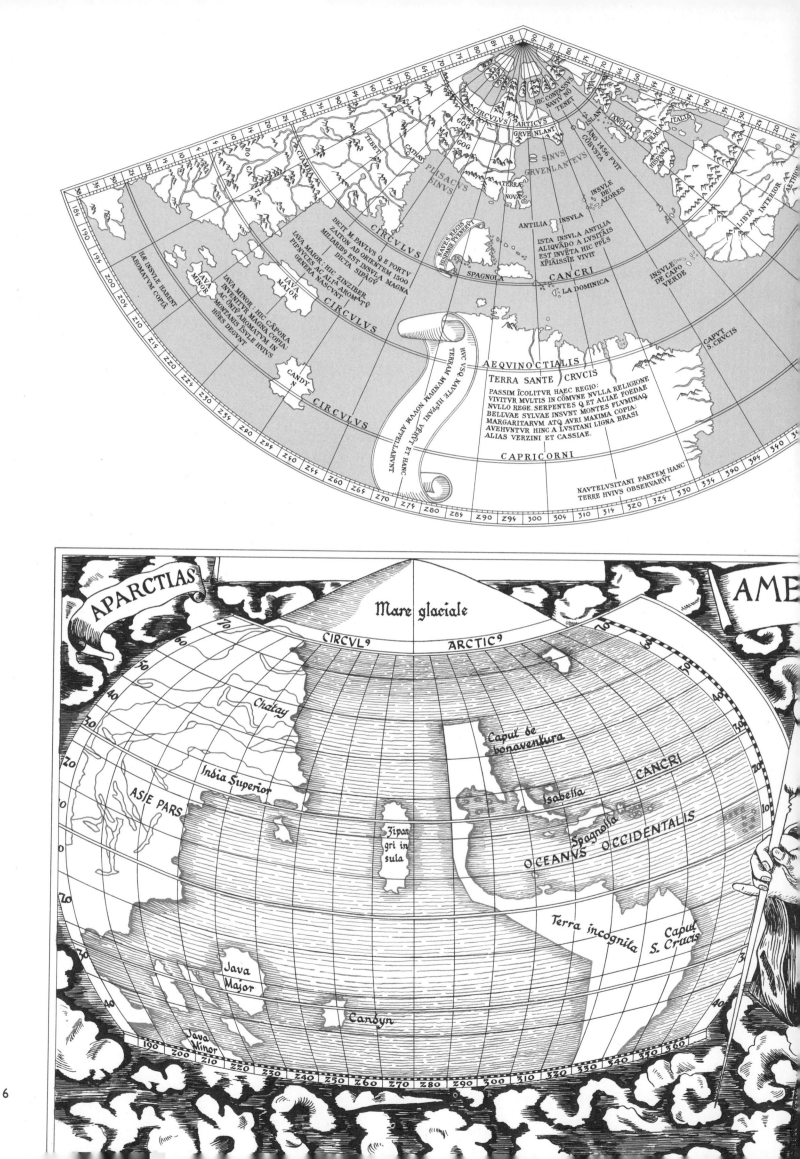

8 Part of Ruysch's Map, 1507

First Impressions of America

When Columbus died in 1506, the significance of his discoveries was still obscure. His own belief and that of many others that Asia and its adjacent islands had been reached is illustrated in the Johannes Ruysch map of 1507. As early as 1502, however, Amerigo Vespucci, another traveller in the New World, had expressed the opinion that this was a separate continent. Martin Waldseemüller's map, published in the same year as that of Ruysch, is the first to be based on Vespucci's theory and the first to apply, in the latter's honour, the name 'America' to the new continent.

9 Part of Waldseemüller's Map, 1507

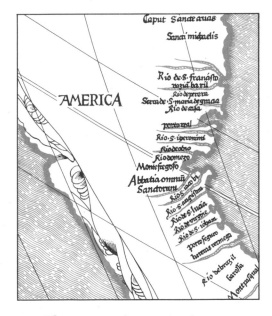

10 The name 'America' appears on a map for the first time

ARCTIC CIRCLE

GREENLAND

ATLANTIC

CORTE-REAL

CAPE
CHIDLEY

JOHN CABOT 1497, GASPAR CORTE-REAL 1500
ALVARES FAGUNDES C-1521, JOHN RUT 1527

OCEAN

Belle I.

Anticosti I.

NEWFOUNDLAND

RUT

FAGUNDES

CAPE
RACE

B A N K S

CAPE
BRETON

CABOT

GRAND
BANK

ESTEVAN GOMEZ
1524-25

CAPE
SABLE

F I S H I N G   Sable I.

CAPE
COD

GIOVANNI DA VERRAZANO 1524

100   0   100   200   300   400

MILES

8

11   Exploration of the North-east Coastline

Records of how the coastline from the Bay of Fundy to Hudson Bay was explored are meagre, and their interpretation has caused much controversy. Expeditions were officially authorized by no less than four governments. Sailing under the English flag were the Genoese John Cabot, his son Sebastian (whose story is especially controversial), and the Englishman John Rut. Gaspar Corte-Real, his brother Miguel, and Alvarez Fagundes served their native Portugal. Giovanni da Verrazano was a Florentine employed by the King of France and Estevan Gomez a Portuguese employed by Spain. There were others as well, and some no doubt about whom no record remains. After the earliest voyages, hope of other Mexicos or Perus rich in gold and silver waned, and the primary objective became to find a way through or north of what seemed an unfortunate obstacle on the route to Asia. Meanwhile, however, the major discovery actually made, the great fishing banks, began immediately to attract increasing numbers of fishermen from England, France, and Portugal.

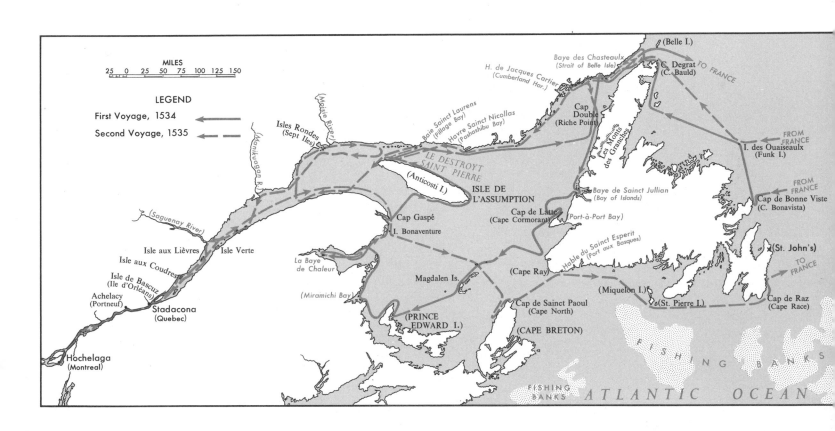

12   The Voyages of Jacques Cartier

The first explorer known to have penetrated much beyond the coastline into what is now Canada was Jacques Cartier. Supported by Francis I of France, Cartier spent the summer of 1534 exploring the Gulf of St. Lawrence, and the following year ascended the St. Lawrence River as far as the Indian villages of Stadacona (Quebec) and Hochelaga (Montreal). After glimpsing the upper reaches of the St. Lawrence and learning of the Ottawa as well, he returned to Stadacona for the winter and thence to France. By this time earlier hopes for a passage through to the Pacific had dimmed, but Indian tales, especially of the Kingdom of the Saguenay, convinced Cartier and Francis I that a rich territory, perhaps in north-eastern Asia, was not much farther up river. Delayed until 1541 by events in Europe, a major expedition under a courtier, the Sieur de Roberval, as military commander and Cartier as chief pilot was sent to establish a colony in Canada as a base for the conquest of the Saguenay. Failure, partly due to quarrelling and bad luck, but inevitable because of the nature of the objective, was followed by a long lull in official French interest in the region.

IL Disegno de discoperto
della nova Franza
Bolognini Zalterij
Anno MD LXVI

13 Part of Zaltieri's Map, 1566

Results of Early Explorations

Maps based on the discoveries made by Cartier and his predecessors were the best available for the next generation or more. The most important was that of the Dutchman, Gerardus Mercator, published in 1569. It introduced for the first time his famous method of map projection, while its American section portrayed accurately the extent of contemporary knowledge of that region. The Venetian map of Bolognino Zaltieri, on the other hand, shows what confusion still existed in many quarters regarding the St. Lawrence. It is a good example, too, of the wishful thinking of the age about a northern route to Asia and about the rumoured Strait of Anian.

From the standpoint of Canadian history, the main results of explorations to this date were: (1) quite full knowledge had been obtained of the Newfoundland-St. Lawrence coastal area with its great fishing banks but lack of rich kingdoms to conquer; (2) it had become almost certain that the Americas were separate from Asia, and that there was no seaway through them. This left only a quickening hope, especially in England, that there might be found a way around to the north better than that which Magellan had discovered to the south. It is noteworthy that the Zaltieri and similar maps were being published just at the time when Sir Humphrey Gilbert became interested in his great and disappointing search for the North-west Passage.

Anno Domino 1500 Gaspar Corterealis
Portogalensis navigavit ad has terras sperans
a parte Septentrionali invenire transitum ad
insulas Moluccas, perveniens autem ad fluvium
quem a deuectic navibus vocant Rio nevada,
propter vigens frigus altius in Septentrionem
pergere desitit perlustravit autem litora
in meridiem usq ad C. Razo.
    Anno 1504 Britones primi invenerant litora
nove Francie circa ostia Sinus S. Laurentii
    Anno 1524 Joannes Verrazzanus Florentinus
nomine regis Gall Francisci primi ex portu
Diepa protectus Martii ad litus meridionale
noue Francie pervenit circum 34 graduum
latitud, atq inde versus orientem omne litus
perlustravit usq ad Britonium promontorium
    Anno 1534 duce classi Jacobo Cartier
lustrata fuit nova Francia & proximo
anno regi Gallie conquiri coepit.

Groenland

Eſtotilant

C. de
terra firma

Golfam de
Merofro

Drogo

Hoc fluvae
facilior eſt
navigatio
in Saguenai

Saguenai

Terra
Corte
realis

Chaſteaux
Belle yſle
C. Blanco di degrad abjs

Honguedo

y. Nes

Noua

Fran
Canada

Sinus

S Laurentij
y della aſsumptione

y. des oiſeaux

Hocheluy

C. de Mommorancy

Terra de
bacalhos

C. de bona viſta

France nauheuz

Hochela ga

G. de Chaleur

J. des liépures

S Pol
S Petro
S Joan

C. de Breton

C. de Razo

Chilaga

J. D'Orleans

Mommorancy

Noro mbega

Eſtane a
terra dus
Bretones

Arredonda

y. de Juan eſteuēz

Norombega

Moco
fa

r. grande

y. de garca

Auac al

Apalchen

C. de arenas

Santana

Juan de ſamp

Iped ra

C. doblado

Calicu az

r. de Flores

rio de pescadores

C S Johan

La Bermuda

OCEANVS ATLANTICVS

Capaſchi

Jugil

La Flo
rida

La emperadada

rio del eſpirito Santo

Toua

C. de Canaueral

Guanahani inſule

Golfo Mexi

cano

Cuba

Tortuga

Hiſpania noua

14 Part of Mercator's Map, 1569

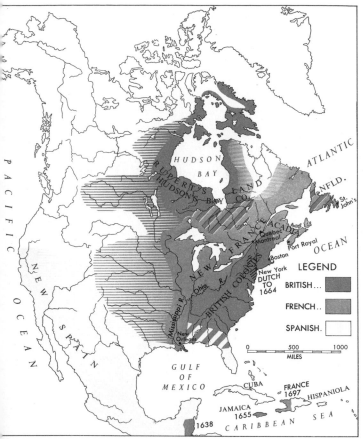

Base map copyright Canadian Aero Service Limited, Ottawa

15 European Spheres of Interest

The seventeenth century was one of rapid development in North America in the course of which the Spaniards consolidated their control in the south and the English established flourishing settlements along the Atlantic coast, while the French colonized with greater difficulty and less success Acadia and the St. Lawrence Valley of Canada. Meanwhile, the four great entries into the interior of the continent were all discovered and opened. The St. Lawrence, the most immediately useful, permitted the French to establish a potentially great inland fur-trading empire, linked just as the century ended with the Mississippi entry as well. The Hudson River, explored by Henry Hudson in 1609, enabled his employers, the Dutch, to create an important agricultural and trading colony which they lost, however, to the English in 1664. Hudson Bay, also explored by Hudson (1610–11) but on behalf this time of his native England, became the centre of Hudson's Bay Company fur-trading after 1670. However, the Company's rights were vigorously disputed by the French who had reached the Bay by land. As the century ended, French-English rivalry over the fur trade of both Hudson Bay and the interior, and over the fisheries of Newfoundland, was becoming a dominant theme in North American history.

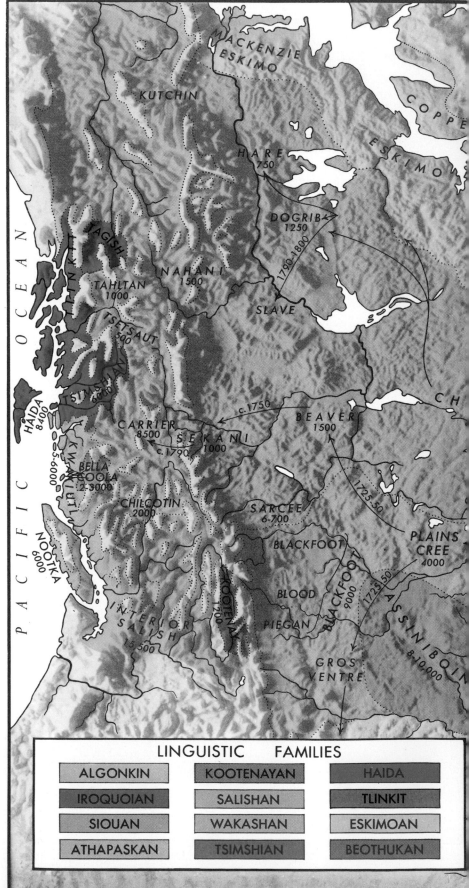

LINGUISTIC   FAMILIES

ALGONKIN	KOOTENAYAN	HAIDA
IROQUOIAN	SALISHAN	TLINKIT
SIOUAN	WAKASHAN	ESKIMOAN
ATHAPASKAN	TSIMSHIAN	BEOTHUKAN

Most of the tribes met during the European penetration of the interior of North America were scattered and nomadic, and our knowledge about them is limited.   The present map, therefore, attempts merely to show: (1) approximate locations of tribes at the time of their first contact with the Europeans, i.e. about the years 1525 east, and 1725 west, of 85° longitude; (2) estimated numbers in each tribe at that time; (3) the direction of certain major tribal migrations; (4) the linguistic grouping of tribes.   This last is of importance as indicating probable earlier associations and movements of what may have become widely separated tribes.   It is important too in making clear that the early explorers and fur traders faced no real language barrier in advancing from tribe to tribe all the way from the Atlantic to Hudson Bay and the foothills of the Rockies, since most of this vast region was occupied by Algonkian peoples.

ENTERING THE INTERIOR

GREENLAND ICE CAP

BYLOT AND BAFFIN 1616

DAVIS 1587

DAVIS 1585

Cape Farew

FROBISHER 1576

FOXE 1631

MUNCK 1619-20

BUTTON 1612-13

JAMES 1631-32

HUDSON 1610-11

Cape Chidley

ATLANTIC

OCEAN

Belle I.

Cape Rac

Cape Breton

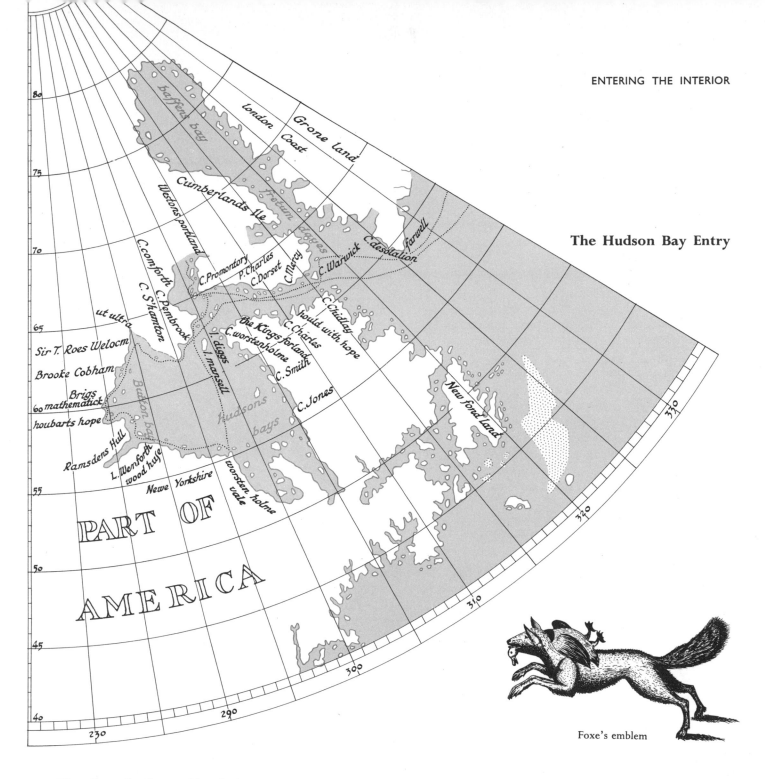

The Hudson Bay Entry

Foxe's emblem

17 The Search for a North-west Passage

Arctic explorers from Martin Frobisher to Foxe and James sought a North-west Passage to Asia, and instead gradually revealed one of the great entries to the North American continent. Except for the Dane, Jens Munck, all were English. The *Discovery*, the first of those famous Arctic ships that have become better known than many of their captains, made at least six of the voyages—under Waymouth in 1602, Hudson on his last great venture in 1610–11, Button in 1612–13, Gibbons in 1614, and Bylot and Baffin in 1615 and again in 1616.

Base map copyright Canadian Aero Service Limited, Ottawa

18 Part of Luke 'North West' Foxe's Map, 1635

The search for a North-west Passage ended for over a century with the rival voyages in 1631 of Luke 'North West' Foxe, a middle-aged seafarer of Hull, and Thomas James of Bristol. Both published books on their return, Foxe's containing his famous map, James' later inspiring Coleridge to write *The Ancient Mariner*.

The St. Lawrence Entry

19 Champlain's Explorations

Samuel de Champlain had visited the West Indies and served at the court of Henry IV of France before entering upon his remarkable career as explorer and colonizer in Acadia and Canada from 1603 until his death in 1635. His own travels included a trip up the St. Lawrence as far as the site of Hochelaga in 1603, investigation of the Bay of Fundy and its vicinity, 1604–7, ventures up the Richelieu into Lake Champlain in 1609 and up the Ottawa to Allumette Island in 1613, and finally a long round-about return journey (1615–16) through the Huron country and down south of Lake Ontario to make an attack on the Iroquois. His young *coureurs de bois* such as Etienne Brulé, Nicolas Vignau, and Jean Nicolet, and missionaries like Father Le Caron, supplied him with additional information. His professional skill as a geographer in piecing all his knowledge together in order to clarify much of the puzzling inter-relationship of the St. Lawrence, Richelieu, Ottawa, and Great Lakes waterways is displayed in his great map of 1632. The earlier map of 1612 shows how much he did not yet know at that time. A comparison of the almost contemporary Luke Foxe and Champlain maps reveals that the English and French were only vaguely familiar with each other's discoveries.

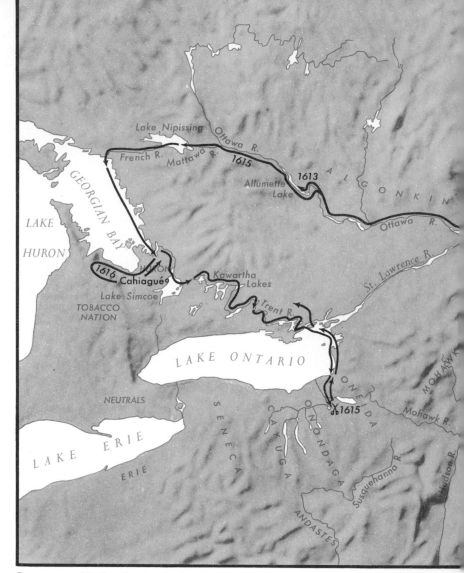

Base map copyright Canadian Aero Service Limited, Ottawa

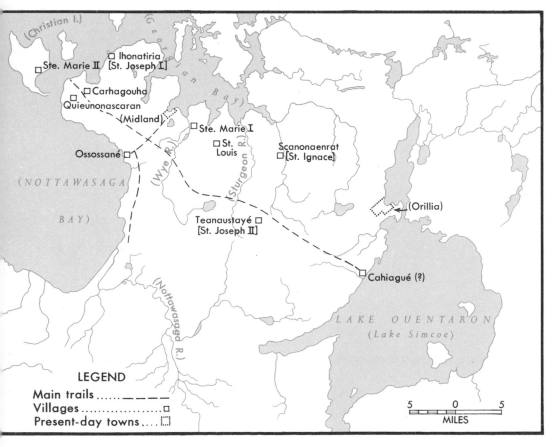

LEGEND

Main trails .... — — —
Villages .... □
Present-day towns ....□

20 Huronia

The Hurons of Champlain's time, numbering perhaps 16,000, lived semi-agricultural lives in some eighteen villages huddled close together between Georgian Bay and Lake Simcoe. The villages were primitive and changed location from time to time for such reasons as the exhaustion of fuel supply and soil in the immediate vicinity. A Recollet, Father Le Caron, preceded Champlain into this region in the summer of 1615. The missionary work thus begun was continued after 1626 by the Jesuits who made a major effort to create a Christian Huronia comparable to the Christian societies they were currently establishing among South American Indians especially in Paraguay. In 1648 and 1649, however, the Huron nation was broken and dispersed by the Iroquois, among those tortured and slain being five Jesuits, including Jean de Brébeuf and Gabriel Lalemant.

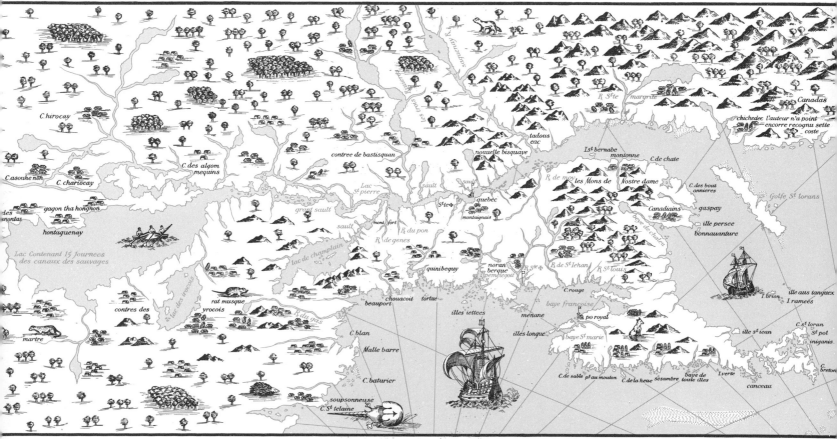

21 Part of Champlain's 1612 Map

ENTERING THE INTERIOR

MER DV NORT GLACIALLE

C. Worsnam

C. Harles

NOUVELLE FRANCE

La Nation des Puans

Isle où il y a une
mine de cuivre

Lac des Biserenis

Sault

Sault

Sault

Sault

Sault

Petite nation des
Algommeguins

Algomme guins

Sault

Sault

Sault

Sault

Les trois rivieres

Sault

quebec

Grande Lac

Sault

Mer douce

Descouvertures de ce grand lac, et de toutes ses terres
depuis le sault S. Louis par le sr de Champlain, es
années 1614, et 1615, iusques en l'an 1618.

Lieu on il y a forse
Cerfs

Hurons

Sault

Sault

Abene
qui

Lac de Champlain

Chouacoit
Port aux Isles

Grande riviere qui vient du
mi dy

Cheueux releuez

Gens de
Petun

Lac St Louis

Sain- tonge

Hiro cois

Cap des Isles
Beau port
Port St Louis

Les gens de feu
assistagueron ons

La nation neutre

Antouoronons

Cap blan
Malle barre

R. aux
escailles

Port fortune

Nation ou il y a quantité de beuffles

Habitation des sauvages
maniganaticou it

Riviere de Champlain

Baye de nostre Dame

Carantouann ais

Riviere
des trettes

Isle de l'Ascension

Virginia

C. Charles

Henry

Carte de la nouvelle france, augmentée depuis la
derniere, servant a la navigation faicte en son vray
Meridien, par le sr de Champlain Capitaine pour le Roy
en la Marine; lequel depuis l'an 1603 iusques en l'année
1629; a descouvert plusieurs costes, terres, lacs, rivieres,
et Nations de sauvages, par cy devant incognuës, comme
il se voit en ses relations qui a faict Imprimer en
1632 ou il se voit cette marque Iɪᵉ ce sont habitations
qu'ont faict les françois.

| 283 | 284 | 285 | 286 | 287 | 288 | 289 | 290 | 291 | 292 | 293 | 294 | 295 | 296 | 297 | 298 | 299 | 300 | 301 | 302 | 303 | 304 | 305 | 306 | 307 | 308 | 309 |

22   Champlain's 1632 Map

Quineannes fort landt

C. Elizabeth

Lomle Inlet

Groenlant dia

Terres de la Brador

Esquimaux Brest Croix blanche

La grande baye Belle isle
Isle fichot
Cap de grat
Cap rouge

Chisdec

Groye

Baye de rochers Le Golphe St Laurens Baye dorge
Sauvages Berfiam iste Les isles aux Chauaux Isle aux apouois
Basse de Ste Marie Port aux Ours Baye blanche
Montagnairs Port neuf C. St Iean
Baye des ballaines Isles des fougues
Les quemain Saincte Margueritte C. des rosiers Anticosty Terre nouve Isle de moy
Tadousac Montane C. dechute Gaspay C. de bonne viste
St Barnabé Monts nostre Dame Isle de bacallos
Le Bic Baye des molues Baye Ste Claire
Isle persee
Isle bonaventure Baye de la Conception
Baye de Chateu Bon des orphelins Isle aux oyseaux Cap Ste Fresaye
Nouvelle France Miscou Cap de ray Frinouse
Tregatay Isle Brion Isles despoirs
La baye du petit misamichy Isle ramee Ste Claire Cap de raze
Etechemins La R Ste Iean La Magdelene St Paul Rocher
C. des mines C. St Laurens Rochers
Ste Croix Isle St Iean Niganis Isles St Pierre Le grand banc
Pemetegoit Cap Enfumé
Baye fran Gransibou
çoise Bane vert
Menane C. de Poitrincourt Cap breton Banquereaux
Souriçois Cap St Antoine
Isle haulte Baye Ste Marie Canceau
Horsaines Ste Margueritte L isle verte Port de savalette
Port de Baye de toute isles
Ste Helaine
Cap fourchu Sesambre
C. de la heve Isle des martires
C. negre Port au mouton
Cap de Sable
Isles aux loups marins Isle de Sable

5 10 20 30 40 50 60 70 80 90 100

Faicte l'an 1632 parle sieur de Champlain

ENTERING THE INTERIOR

HUDSON
BAY

JAMES
BAY

ROCKY MOUNTAINS

North Saskatchewan R.

HENDAY 1754-55

Red Deer R.

South Saskatchewan R.

Yellowstone R.

Missouri R.

Churchill R.

Nelson R.

KELSEY 1690

York Fort

Fort Severn

Fort Paskoiac

KELSEY
1690-92
Route uncertain

Lake
Winnipegosis

Fort Dauphin

Lake
Manitoba

LAKE
WINNIPEG

LA VERENDRYE 1742-43

Fort la Reine

Fort Maurepas

Fort Rouge

Fort St Charles

Red R.

Fort St Pierre

Lake
of the Woods

Rainy
Lake

Grand Portage

Charlton
I.

Fort
Albany

Moose Fort

Charles Fort

ST. SIMON AND
ALBANEL 16

Albany R.

Abitibi R.

Eastmain

Rupert R.

L. Nipigon

Fort Ste Anne

Fort Kaministiquia

LAKE SUPERIOR

Black
Hills

Mississippi R.

Fort Chequamegon

Chequamegon
Bay

Fort Ste Croix

Green
Bay

Fort le Sueur

Fort St Antoine

Fort Beauharnois

Fort Trempealeau

Fort St Nicolas

JOLLIET AND
MARQUETTE
1673

JOLLIET AND MARQUETTE 1673

L. MICHIGAN

Sault Ste Marie
1672

St Ignace

Fort
Michilimackinac

L. HURON

DOLLIER AND
GALINÉE

Ottawa R.

St. Lawr

Fort Frontenac
(Cataraqui)

DOLLIER AND GALINEE 1669

L. ONTARIO

Fort
Osw

1670

Detroit

L. ERIE

DOLLIER AND
GALINEE 1669

Fort Le Boeuf

JOLLIET AND MARQUETTE

Fort St Joseph

Fort Miami

Fort St Louis

Fort Crèvecoeur

LA SALLE
1682

Fort
Vincennes

Fort Ouiatanon

Wabash R.

VIELE 1692-94

Ohio R.

Fort Duquesne

APPALACHIAN MOUNTAIN

Missouri R.

S. Platte R.

Fort
Orléans

St Louis

Cahokia

Fort de Chartres

Kaskaskia

Fort Massiac

JOLLIET AND MARQUETTE 1673

Arkansas R.

1682

LA SALLE

Tennessee R.

Jamestown

COUTURE 1699-1700

Savannah R.

Charleston

Mississippi R.

LA SALLE

Fort

Fort St Pierre

Fort

Mobile o

New Orleans

1687

1685-86

LA SALLE
1684

Rio Grande

Trinity R.

GULF OF MEXICO

LEGEND

Explorations
Forts
Mountainous areas

French   English

100   0   100   200   300   400

MILES

PART TWO   EXPLORATION AND DEVELOPMENT TO 1763

SECTION 3   GROWTH AND CONFLICT

23 Exploration and Fur Trade in the Interior

Champlain, having founded Quebec in 1608 and nursed it through its infancy, was obliged to surrender it in 1629 to an English force under David Kirke and was not able to return until after the restoration of peace in 1632. Meanwhile, in Acadia, the long conflict between English and French had begun even earlier with Samuel Argall's raids on French settlements in 1613 and James I's grant of 'Nova Scotia' to Sir William Alexander in 1621. In 1759, one hundred and thirty years after Kirke, Wolfe captured Quebec again, bringing the struggle to its culmination. Finally with peace in 1763 Canada and adjacent possessions were transferred to British rule.

The long-standing hostility of France and Britain in Europe and other parts of the world was heightened in North America by rivalry over the Newfoundland fisheries and the fur trade of the continental interior. With regard to the latter the French, following the example of Champlain and encouraged by missionary zeal and inviting waterways branching inward from Montreal, took an early lead. During the seventeenth century they not only explored the whole Great Lake region but reached out as well to Hudson Bay and the mouth of the Mississippi. The curbing of the Iroquois in 1666 by the Marquis de Tracy cleared the way for especially rapid progress after that date, stimulated by Colbert, Talon, and Frontenac. In the eighteenth century, the La Vérendryes and others led the way out into the Great Plains.

The English were comparatively slow in pushing inland from Hudson Bay or the Atlantic seaboard, and what they did accomplish was sometimes with the assistance of renegade Frenchmen like Radisson and Jean Couture and Dutchmen like Viele. Geographic and other factors, however, made their fur traders, whether operating from Hudson Bay or the Hudson River, dangerous competitors of the more energetic French. Only a few representative and reasonably well-recorded journeys can be shown with advantage on a map, but this must not be allowed to obscure the importance of Radisson, Groseilliers, Dulhut, Tonti, and countless others—missionaries, *coureurs de bois,* and Indian guides, many completely unknown to history—who played their part in the discovery of the continent.

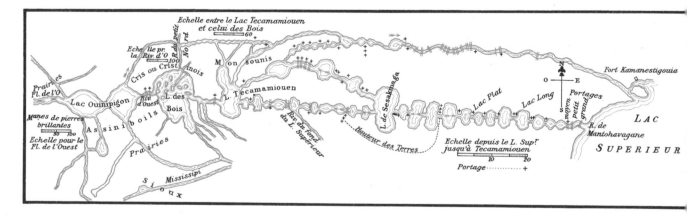

24 The Ochagach Map

Some of the problems of the explorers can be understood when the map of La Vérendrye's Indian guide Ochagach is compared with the modern representation of the waterways between Lake Superior and Lake Winnipeg included in Map 23 and in greater detail in Map 62. Ochagach was probably superior to most savage guides, but he was typically vague about distance and direction and hopeful in his assurances that La Vérendrye would find the westward-flowing rivers he sought and also mountains of shining stones.

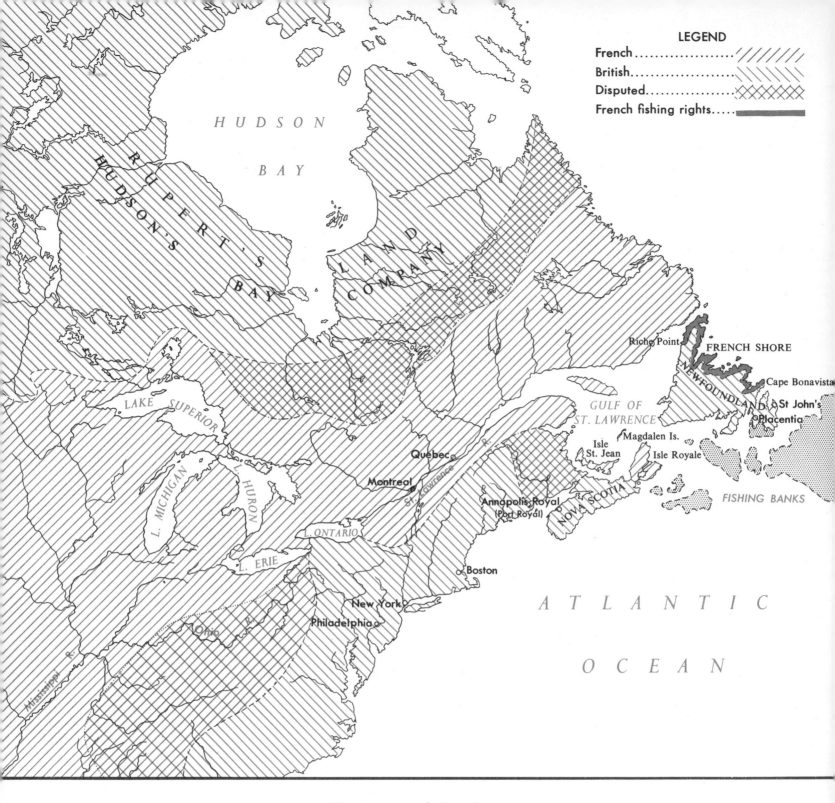

25 The Treaty of Utrecht, 1713

France's first permanent territorial losses in North America were acknowledged in the Treaty of Utrecht which ended the War of the Spanish Succession (Queen Anne's War) in 1713. By it France recognized British ownership of the Hudson Bay region, Newfoundland, and 'all Nova Scotia or Acadie, with its ancient boundaries, as also the city of Port Royal'. Specifically retained by France were the islands of the Gulf of St. Lawrence including Isle Royale (Cape Breton) and also certain fishing rights along the northward shores of Newfoundland be-tween Cape Bonavista and Riche Point. The special interests of both countries in respect to the territories of their Indian allies were admitted, the Iroquois territories being definitely assigned to the British sphere. A provision that commissioners be appointed to determine the various boundaries more exactly proved ineffective, and when the next war began the limits of the Hudson's Bay Territories remained in dispute and French occupation of what is now New Brunswick still continued.

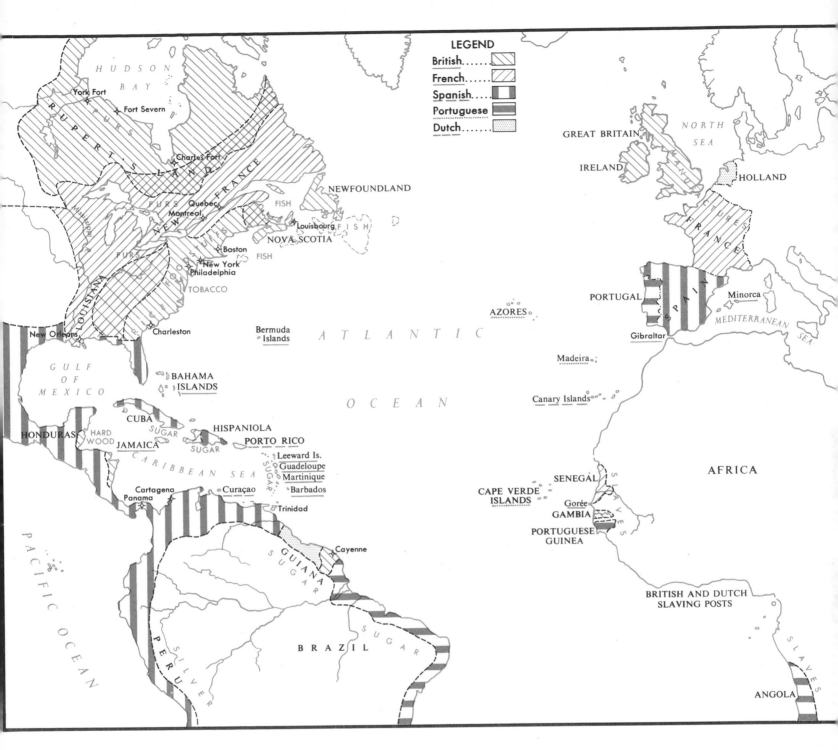

26 Atlantic Trading Rivalries

Eighteenth-century wars between Britain and France were by no means confined to border clashes in North America. They were world-wide struggles for commercial and colonial supremacy, fought in eastern oceans and India as well as in Europe and the Atlantic region. In the latter the furs and fish of Canada were among the principal prizes at stake, along with the sugar of the West Indies and the slave trade of Africa.

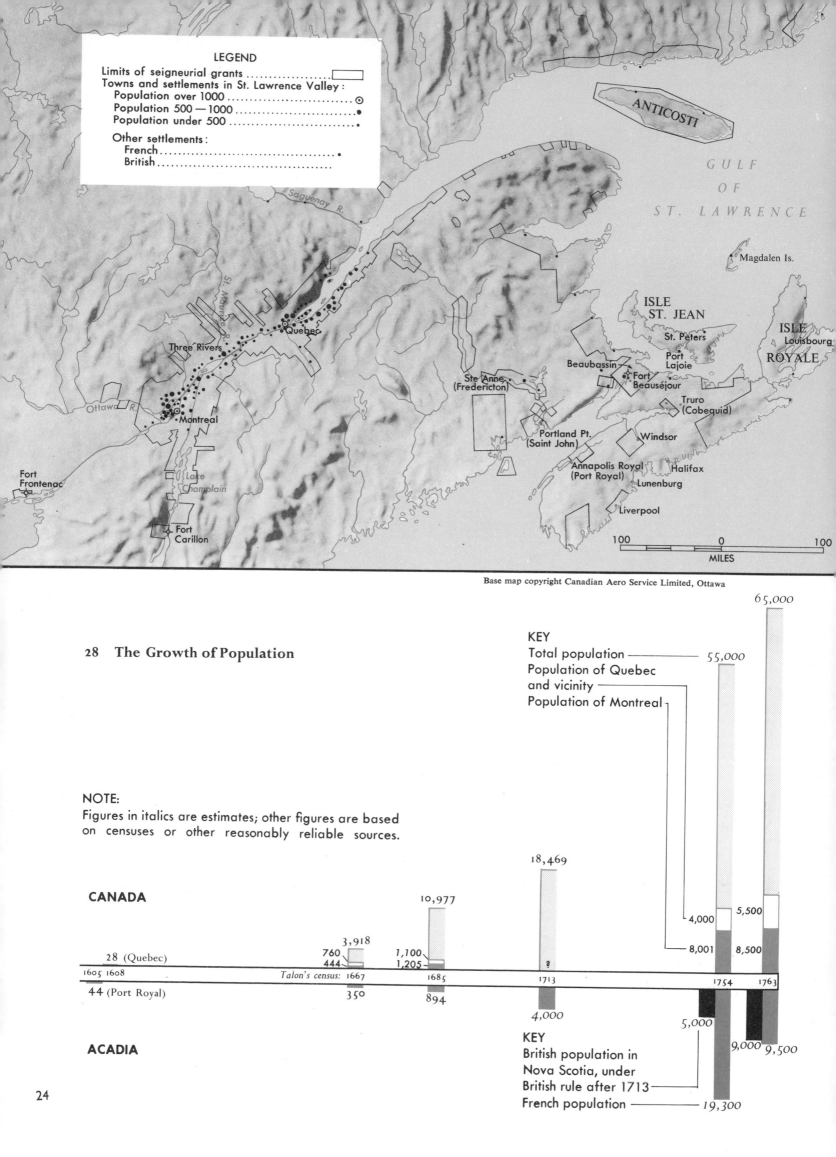

LEGEND

Limits of seigneurial grants .... ☐
Towns and settlements in St. Lawrence Valley :
    Population over 1000 .... ⊙
    Population 500 — 1000 .... •
    Population under 500 .... •

Other settlements :
    French .... •
    British ....

Base map copyright Canadian Aero Service Limited, Ottawa

28 The Growth of Population

KEY
Total population ————— 65,000
Population of Quebec
and vicinity —
Population of Montreal

NOTE:
Figures in italics are estimates; other figures are based
on censuses or other reasonably reliable sources.

CANADA

28 (Quebec)

44 (Port Royal)

KEY
British population in
Nova Scotia, under
British rule after 1713 —
French population ————— 19,300

ACADIA

24

A major disadvantage of the French in North America was the extent to which they were outnumbered by the British to the south. The spectacular achievements of their fur traders and explorers were not matched by their 'habitant' farmers who were adding only slowly to the area under cultivation in the St. Lawrence lowlands of Canada and in a few parts of Acadia, notably on the tidal marshlands at the head of the Bay of Fundy, on Isle St. Jean (Prince Edward Island), and around Port Royal.

The land-holding system was seigneurial, based on that of France. Grants of some sixty seigneuries had been made before 1663; more than that number followed rapidly during the next nine years when Jean Talon was intendant, and others were added during the remainder of the French régime and even in a few cases after the British conquest. The last grant was in 1788, and the system was abolished in 1854. Seigneurs were supposed to see to the clearing and settlement of their land, but few were able to satisfy fully these requirements, especially in the early days.

Settlement clung to the coasts and river banks for ease of transportation. The market for farm products, however, was never great —the supply of a few towns and some fishermen and fur traders—although in later years of mounting wars with the British it expanded in line with the needs of reinforced garrisons at Quebec, Louisbourg, Beauséjour, and other forts. Shipbuilding and the productive but unprofitable iron forges on the St. Maurice near Three Rivers were the only significant secondary industries, apart from home spinning and weaving and local milling. The fur trade itself, however colourful, was always an uncertain source of wealth and employment. All of this contrasted alarmingly with the rapid and solid progress of the British colonies.

Population records for the French régime are amazingly detailed and show that growth was very slow before 1663. A period of more rapid expansion followed, due mainly to the efforts of Jean Talon, intendant from 1663 to 1672, and to the support he received from his masters, Louis XIV and Colbert. In the eighteenth century progress continued at a steady but by no means spectacular pace. The total French population (Canadian and Acadian) was still less than 80,000 in 1763 and seemed very small indeed when compared with the 1,500,000 in the British colonies to the south. The largest towns, Quebec and Montreal, were similarly dwarfed by Boston, New York, and Philadelphia.

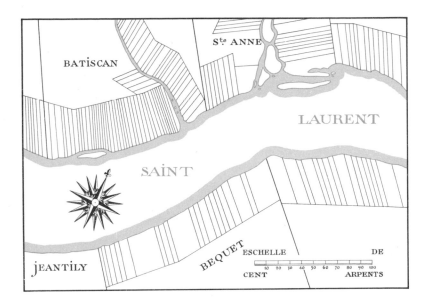

29 The Customary Strip Farms

The farms into which the seigneuries were divided customarily took the form of narrow strips of land so that each could have its own river frontage and its own woodlot in back. The habitants lived, as a result, in *côtes* or scattered lines of houses along the river banks. To suggest the advantage of more compact communities in the traditional French pattern, Talon founded three 'round' villages near Quebec, but his example was not followed.

GROWTH
AND CONFLICT

30 Talon's Round Villages

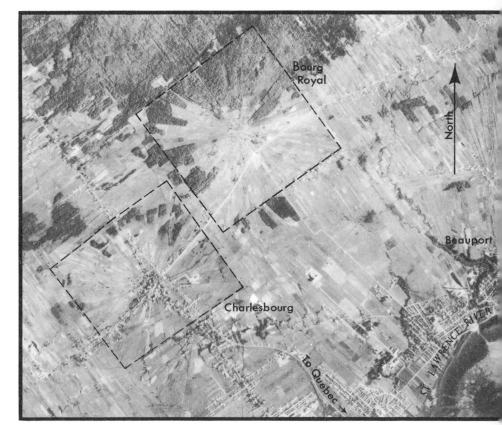

Royal Canadian Air Force photograph

31   The Seven Years' War

The finally decisive struggle between the French and British in North America was the Seven Years' War. In 1754, two years before the formal declaration of war in Europe, conflict began in North America when the French from Canada and the English from Virginia clashed in rival attempts to occupy the rich Ohio Valley. The French built Fort Duquesne at the strategic forks of the Ohio, where the Allegheny and the Monongahela come together, and forced the surrender of a small English expedition under George Washington at nearby Fort Necessity (July 3). For the next five years, except when winter pre-

vented all but minor skirmishes, fighting continued usually on all three fronts: (1) in the west, in the Ohio country and around Lake Erie and Lake Ontario; (2) in the centre, where the Hudson-Champlain-Richelieu waterway constituted the great 'warpath of nations'; and (3) in the north-eastward approaches to Canada, the St. Lawrence gulf and river region.

The main events were as follows:
1755. In the west, the British commander-in-chief, Braddock, was ambushed and defeated approaching Fort Duquesne (July 9); in the centre, the British were victorious in fighting beside Lake George (September 8)

but failed in their object of capturing Fort St. Frédéric (Crown Point); in the east, they captured Fort Beauséjour (June 16) and expelled the Acadians. That autumn the French began building Fort Carillon (Ticonderoga) and the English Fort William Henry and Fort Edward.
1756. England formally declared war on France (May 17). Montcalm, the new French commander-in-chief, captured and destroyed Fort Oswego (Chouagen) on August 14.
1757. Montcalm's capture of Fort William Henry (August 9) was followed by the Indian massacre of many of its garrison and inhabitants.

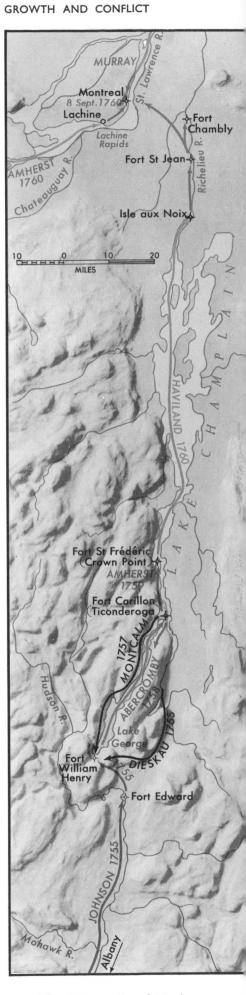

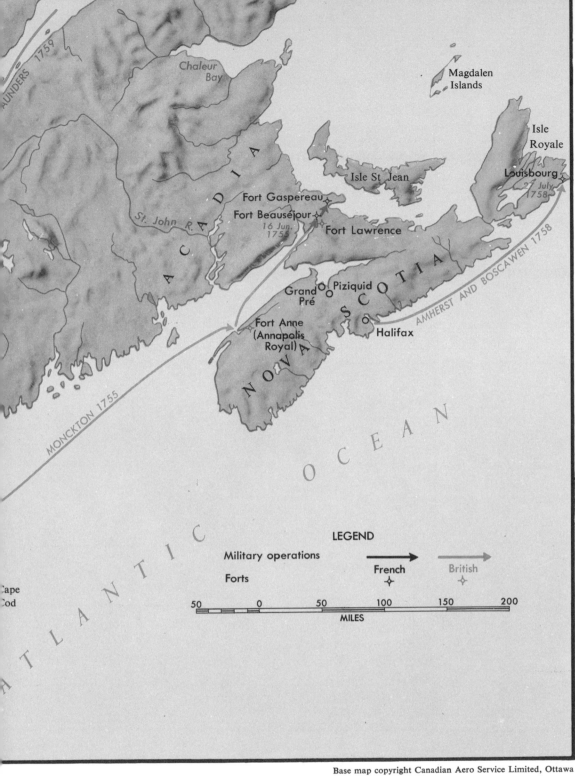

Base map copyright Canadian Aero Service Limited, Ottawa

LEGEND

Military operations

Forts

French →

British →

MILES

1758. Abercromby was repulsed in a major attack on Fort Carillon (July 8), but Amherst, Wolfe, and Admiral Boscawen captured Louisbourg (July 27), Bradstreet raided and destroyed Fort Frontenac (August 25), and Forbes forced the French evacuation of Fort Duquesne (November 23).

1759. The British captured Fort Niagara (July 25) and obliged the French to withdraw without fighting from Fort Carillon (July 26) and Fort St. Frédéric (August 4). But for Amherst's caution, the British advance might have continued as far as Montreal in the weeks that followed. Meanwhile, in the St. Lawrence region,

Admiral Saunders' fleet had succeeded in transporting Wolfe's army to Quebec (June 27) where, after a long summer's siege, it won the Battle of the Plains of Abraham (September 13) and entered the city (September 18).

1760. A brave attempt by Lévis to recapture Quebec led to a British defeat in the Battle of Ste. Foy (April 28), after which Murray retired behind the city walls and withstood siege until the British fleet arrived (May 9–16). Murray, Amherst, and Haviland then converged on Montreal where the final capitulation of New France took place (September 8).

32   The Warpath of Nations

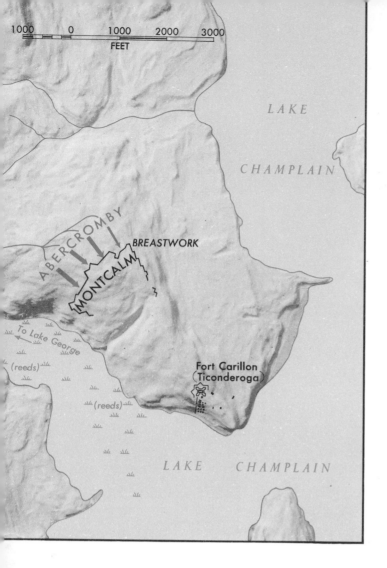

33 Defence of Fort Carillon

Because of the disrepair of Fort Carillon, Montcalm hastily erected advance defences of earthworks surmounted by felled trees, and from these repulsed with smaller numbers a frontal assault prematurely launched by the incompetent Abercromby.

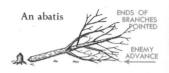

An abatis

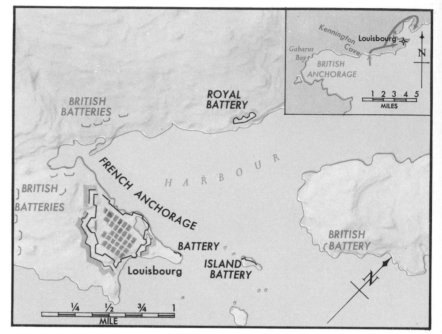

34 Siege of Louisbourg

After a feebly resisted landing in Gabarus Bay (June 8) and in spite of difficult swampy approaches and French sorties, the British succeeded, with much effort, in placing themselves in position to bombard Louisbourg from several points on land as well as from the ships of their fleet. Pounded for eight days by heavy fire and reduced to ruin, the fort surrendered to Amherst (July 27).

35 Siege of Quebec

With Saunders' fleet safely anchored in the shelter of the Island of Orleans (June 27), Wolfe proceeded to establish three camps—a base camp on the island itself, a bombardment site at Point Lévis opposite Quebec, and his own headquarters north-east of the Montmorency River. After much vacillation he launched a major attack (July 31) in an attempt to force a way through to Quebec along the Beauport shore. Repulsed by the French holding the precipitous Montmorency Heights, he decided finally, with the approach of autumn, to take his brigadiers' advice to slip past Quebec and at least cut the French line of food supply from the west. In fact, surprise, on which the plan depended, was complete, and after the landing at Anse au Foulon and a brisk battle on the Plains of Abraham (September 13) in which he and Montcalm were both fatally wounded, the city was taken (September 18).

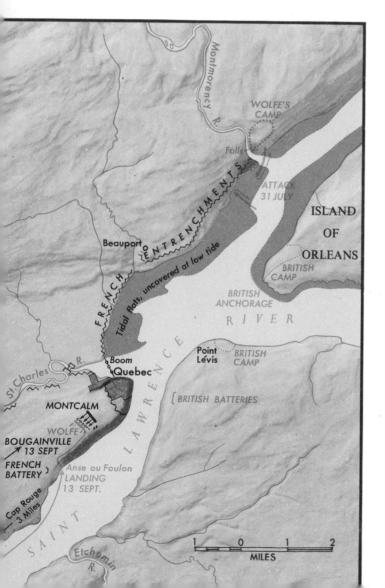

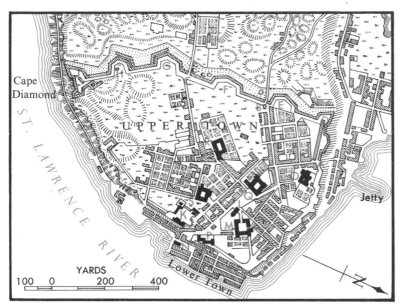

36–37 Quebec, 1763

A Palace Gate
B St. John's Gate
C St. Louis Gate
D Potasse Bastion
E St. John's Bastion
F Ste. Ursule Bastion
G St. Louis Bastion
H La Glacière Bastion
J Cape Diamond Bastion
K Fort St. Louis
L The Cathedral (in ruins)
M The Seminary
N Church of the Lower Town (Notre Dame des Victoires)
O Hôtel Dieu
P The Bishop's Palace
Q The Jesuits
R The Ursulines
S The Recollets

GROWTH AND CONFLICT

38–39 Montreal, 1763

A Parish Church
B Sulpician Seminary
C The Jesuits
D Sisters of the Congregation
E Their hospital
F The Recollets
G Hôtel Dieu
H The Fort
J Arsenal
K Governor's House and Parade
L The Market
M Powder Magazine
N Sally port
O Water Gate
P St. Mary's Gate
Q Market Gate
R The Small Gate
S Recollets' Gate

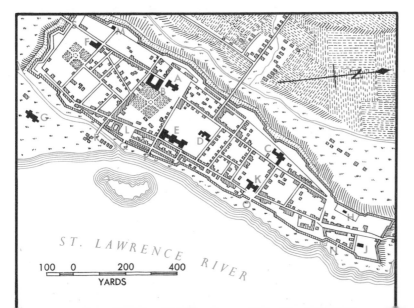

40   The Treaty of Paris, 1763

The Treaty of Paris, signed by Great Britain, France, Spain, and Portugal on February 10, 1763, ended the West European and colonial phases of the Seven Years War, and marked the withdrawal of France from the mainland of North America. In the north-eastern part of the continent, France ceded to Britain all territories that had remained to her after the Treaty of Utrecht, i.e. Canada and what is now New Brunswick, together with adjacent islands, including Isle Royale (Cape Breton) and Isle St. Jean (Prince Edward Island). She retained the fishing rights in Newfoundland guaranteed by the Treaty of Utrecht, and received as well the islands of St. Pierre and Miquelon for use as unfortified fishing bases. In the centre and south, France and Spain gave up all their territories east of the Mississippi from the Great Lakes to Florida, except New Orleans. The latter and French lands west of the Mississippi (Louisiana) had already been transferred to Spain by the secret Treaty of San Ildefonso (November 3, 1762).

Various West Indian islands were restored to their previous owners. The general effect of the treaty was that for a time after 1763, Britain was in possession of the whole eastern half of the continent, France was virtually eliminated as a North American power, and the somewhat enlarged Spanish territories became concentrated in the south-west. The north-west remained as yet almost unknown, except for recent Russian advances down the Alaskan coast.

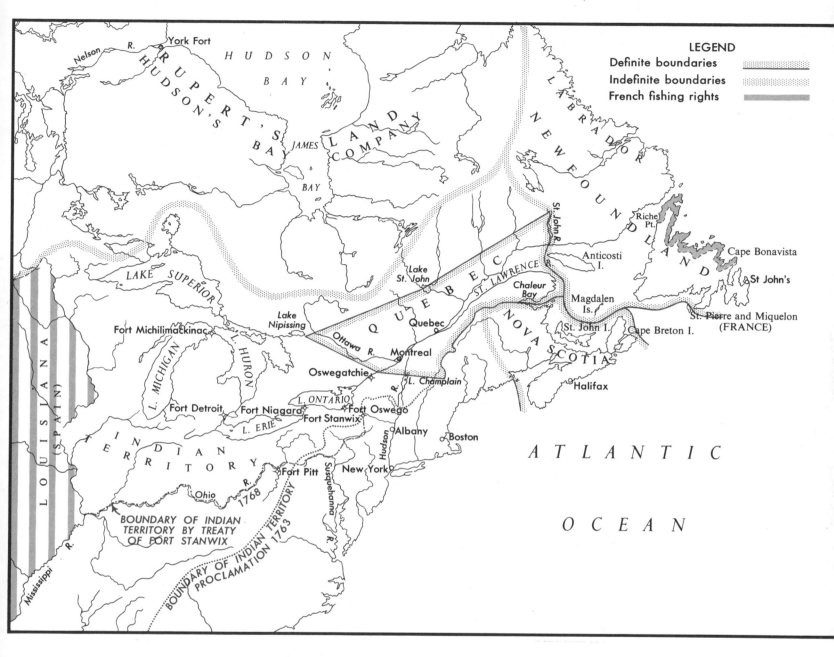

41 The Royal Proclamation of 1763

On October 7, 1763, the Government of George III issued a Proclamation establishing the boundaries and governments of territories acquired in the Treaty of Paris. It (1) created a new colony, Quebec, whose boundary followed Quebec's St. John River, passed from its headwaters through Lake St. John to Lake Nipissing and to the St. Lawrence at the 45th parallel just above Montreal, then turned back eastward along that parallel, the height of land, and along the north shore of Chaleur Bay, as does the present boundary of the Province of Quebec, and crossed west of Anticosti to the mouth of the St. John River; (2) assumed that Nova Scotia included what is now New Brunswick (as Britain had claimed unsuccessfully since 1713) and added to it Cape Breton and St. Jean or St. John (later Prince Edward) Islands; (3) annexed to Newfoundland the coast of Labrador from the St. John River to Hudson Strait and also Anticosti and the Magdalen Islands in order to assure unified control of the gulf and coastal fisheries, these being considered 'the most obvious advantages arising from the Cessions'; (4) set aside all lands west and north of rivers flowing into the Atlantic, except those already granted to the Hudson's Bay Company or included in Quebec, to be Indian Territories from which settlement would be excluded and in which trade could be carried on only under licence. In the next few years, several Indian treaties, notably that with the Iroquois at Fort Stanwix (1768) took the limits of settlement slightly westward.

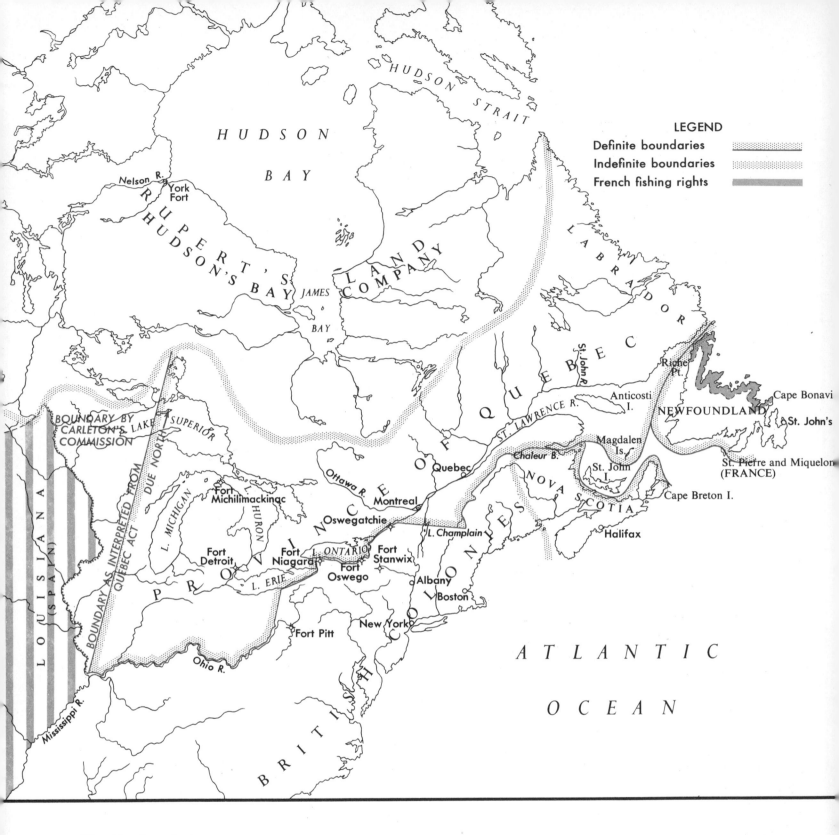

42 The Quebec Act, 1774

The Quebec Act, May 20, 1774, brought both the fisheries of the Gulf of St. Lawrence and the fur trade of the interior within the jurisdiction of the Quebec Government by annexing to that province (1) Labrador, Anticosti, and the Magdalen Islands, previously belonging to Newfoundland, and (2) the Indian Territories south-westward to the junction of the Ohio and Mississippi and thence 'Northward to the Southern Boundary' of the Hudson's Bay Company's lands.

This second provision, although followed by specific provisions to safeguard existing boundaries and rights of the older British colonies, added nevertheless to their growing discontent by limiting their further westward expansion. Moreover, Guy Carleton's commission as governor of Quebec some months later defined the boundary from the Ohio as running northward along the Mississippi, and thus placed it farther west than if it had run due northward. A century later this

apparent discrepancy, clearly unintentional and due to careless wording of the final draft of the Act, led to a vigorous boundary dispute between Manitoba and Ontario, finally decided in favour of the latter by the Judicial Committee of the Privy Council in 1884 (see Maps 97 and 98). Meanwhile St. John Island (Prince Edward Island after 1799) was given separate government in 1769 at the request of the proprietors among whom it had been divided in 1767 (see Map 78).

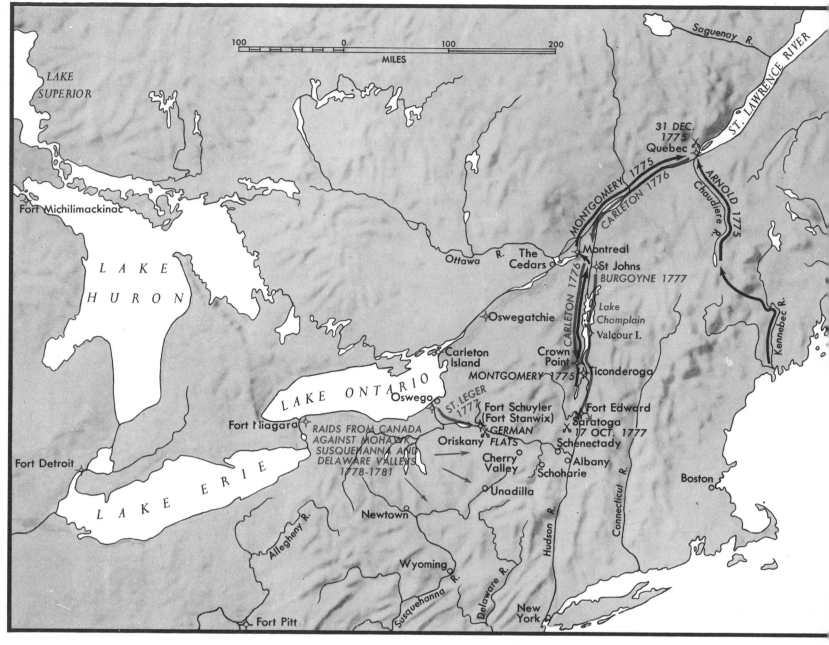

43 The American Revolutionary War, 1775–83

The first shots of the American Revolutionary War at Lexington and Concord (April 19, 1775) near Boston were followed by an attempt to win over the traditional enemy, Canada, first by an appeal from the Second Continental Congress and then by invasion. The invasion, a two-pronged attack led by Richard Montgomery and Benedict Arnold, was the main event of the first year of war apart from the Battle of Bunker Hill. After the heroic defence and final surrender of St. Johns (September 4–November 3), it culminated in an unsuccessful assault on Quebec during which Montgomery was killed (December 31, 1775). When British ships appeared in the spring, the American retreat began, enabling Carleton to recover all of Canada in the summer of 1776 and

advance as far as Crown Point before returning to St. Johns to winter. Meanwhile, a feeble attempt by Americans and their sympathizers to capture Fort Cumberland (Beauséjour) in November, 1776, was repulsed without difficulty. In 1777, Burgoyne's campaign down the Lake Champlain route ended in his disastrous surrender at Saratoga (October 17) when Howe, instead of advancing to his support up the Hudson from New York, turned southward to capture Philadelphia and when St. Leger and his Indian and militia allies were halted before Fort Schuyler (Stanwix). The following years saw little action in the north except for privateering in the Atlantic coast and raids in the Mohawk Valley intended to interfere with the supply of food to Washington's army.

44 Fort Cumberland

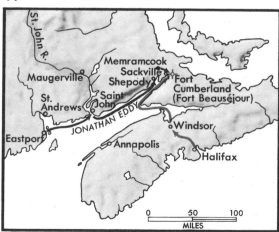

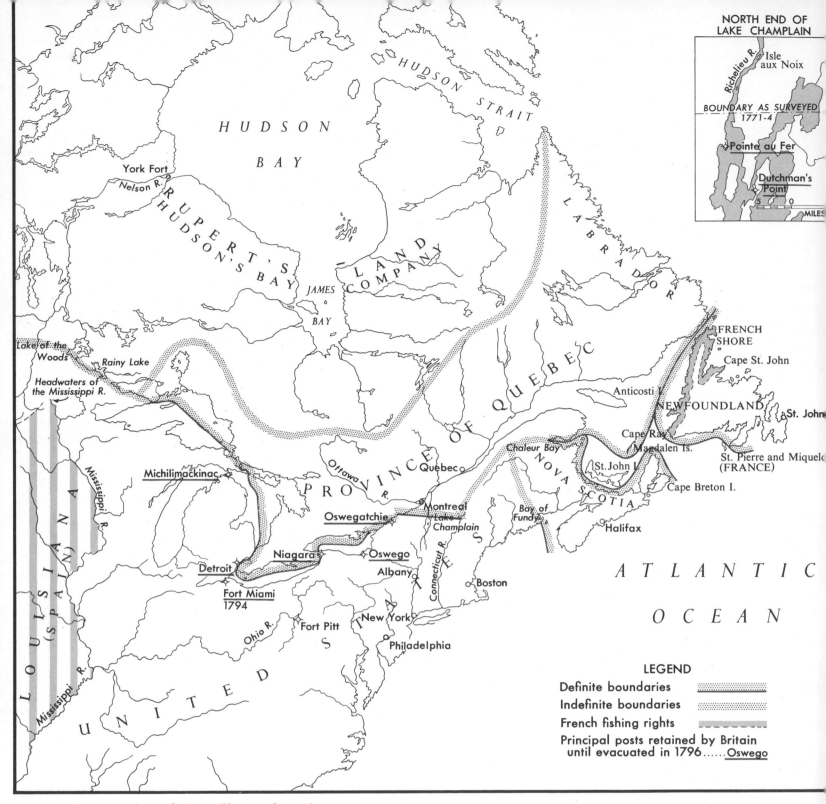

Isle
aux Noix

BOUNDARY AS SURVEYED
1771-4

Pointe au Fer

Dutchman's
Point

MILES

HUDSON STRAIT

HUDSON
BAY

RUPERT'S
HUDSON'S BAY

LAND
COMPANY

JAMES
BAY

LABRADOR

York Fort
Nelson R.

Lake of the
Woods
Rainy Lake

Headwaters of
the Mississippi R.

FRENCH
SHORE
Cape St. John

Anticosti I.
NEWFOUNDLAND
St. John

Cape Ray
Magdalen Is.

PROVINCE OF QUEBEC

St. Pierre and Miquelo
(FRANCE)

Chaleur Bay

Michilimackinac

Ottawa R.

Quebec

NOVA SCOTIA

St. John I.

Cape Breton I.

LOUISIANA (SPAIN)

Mississippi R.

Oswegatchie

Montreal
Lake
Champlain

Bay of
Fundy

Halifax

Niagara

Oswego

Albany

Connecticut R.

ATLANTIC

Detroit

UNITED STATES

Boston

OCEAN

Fort Miami
1794

Ohio R.

Fort Pitt

New York

Mississippi R.

Philadelphia

LEGEND
Definite boundaries
Indefinite boundaries
French fishing rights
Principal posts retained by Britain
     until evacuated in 1796......Oswego

45   The Treaties of Versailles and Paris, 1783

Several treaties signed simultaneously on September 3, 1783, ended the American Revolutionary War and the world-wide conflicts that had arisen from it. Two concerned British North America:

The Treaty of Versailles between Britain and France altered the provisions of the Treaty of Paris (1763) by making France's ownership of St. Pierre and Miquelon unconditional and by adjusting French fishing rights on the northward and eastern shores of Newfoundland to make them lie between Cape St. John and Cape Ray instead of

Cape Bonavista and Riche Point. In a special 'Declaration' that formed part of the agreement, the British Government undertook additionally to prevent its subjects from establishing fixed settlements along the 'French shore', thus virtually eliminating British use of almost half the island.

The Treaty of Paris between Britain and the United States, defining the new relationship of each to the other, included provision that the boundary between the United States and continuing British colonies to the north

should run from the Bay of Fundy up the middle of the St. Croix River to its source, due north to the watershed between the St. Lawrence and the Atlantic, along the watershed to the north-westernmost head of the Connecticut River, down this to the 45th parallel, west along the parallel to the St. Lawrence, up the middle of that and other rivers and lakes to Lake Superior, Rainy Lake, and the Lake of the Woods, across the latter to its most north-western point, and finally due west to the Mississippi. In general this line was to constitute the per-

A xebec on Lake Ontario

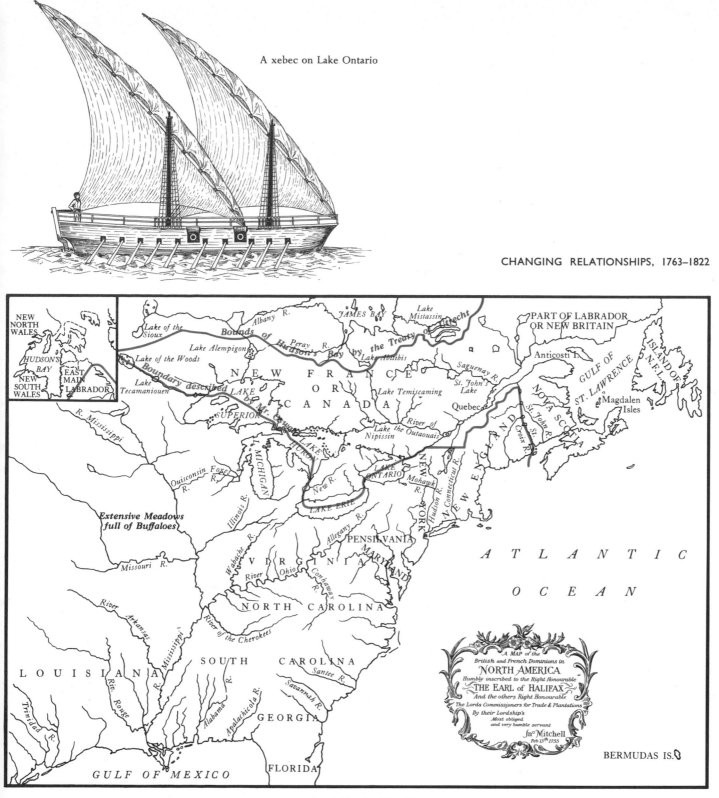

46   Mitchell's Map

manent boundary settlement, but several sections became subjects of controversy when the inadequacies of Mitchell's Map were discovered.   In an attempt to remove these and other sources of discord, such as Britain's retention of important military and fur trading posts on American territory, Jay's Treaty was signed November 19, 1794.   Its results included British withdrawal from the posts during 1796 and a decision by a joint commission as to which was meant by the St. Croix River.   Other boundary problems remained for later solution.

Peace negotiators at Paris, bringing an end to the American Revolutionary War and defining the boundaries of the new United States, relied heavily on a map prepared for the British Government in 1755 by John Mitchell.   A number of boundary problems were to arise from the fact, revealed by later exploration, that Mitchell's map contained important inaccuracies.

Newfoundland was highly important during the mercantile period because of its fishery, and the population increased to about 20,000 by the end of the eighteenth century in spite of earlier official attempts to prevent permanent settlement. Nova Scotia, British since 1713, attracted few new settlers before the founding of Halifax in 1749 when several thousand were brought out from England. Germans and some French and Swiss followed shortly, moving down the coast to Lunenburg. The conquest of France's remaining territories in North America and their retention by the Treaty of 1763 brought British merchants and garrisons to Quebec and Montreal, and groups of farmers migrated

from New England and directly from Britain to various places in the Maritimes.

However, it was the coming of the Loyalists, the refugees of the American Revolutionary War, that first foreshadowed an eventual British majority over the French in British North America. Estimates are that almost 20,000 settled finally in Nova Scotia, 14,000 in New Brunswick, 600 in Isle St. John, 400 in Cape Breton Island, 1,000 in Lower Canada and 6,000 in Upper Canada. The Maritimes group came mainly by ship from New York in 1783, many landing at Port Roseway (renamed Shelburne), temporarily the largest urban centre in British North America. Most soon went on to Halifax,

the Annapolis Valley, or across the Bay of Fundy to the St. John River Valley and its tributaries. Among the latter were several disbanded Loyalist corps and two Scottish regiments. The Quebec Loyalists, arriving more gradually by land, were forbidden by Haldimand, the governor, to settle in the vacant triangle beside the American border (later the Eastern Townships) or in the old French seigneuries except in the immediate vicinity of the refugee camp at William Henry (Sorel). Civilians and some military units spread out therefore along the waterfront from Lake St. Francis to beyond Cataraqui (Kingston). Farther west Joseph Brant's Iroquois received land along the

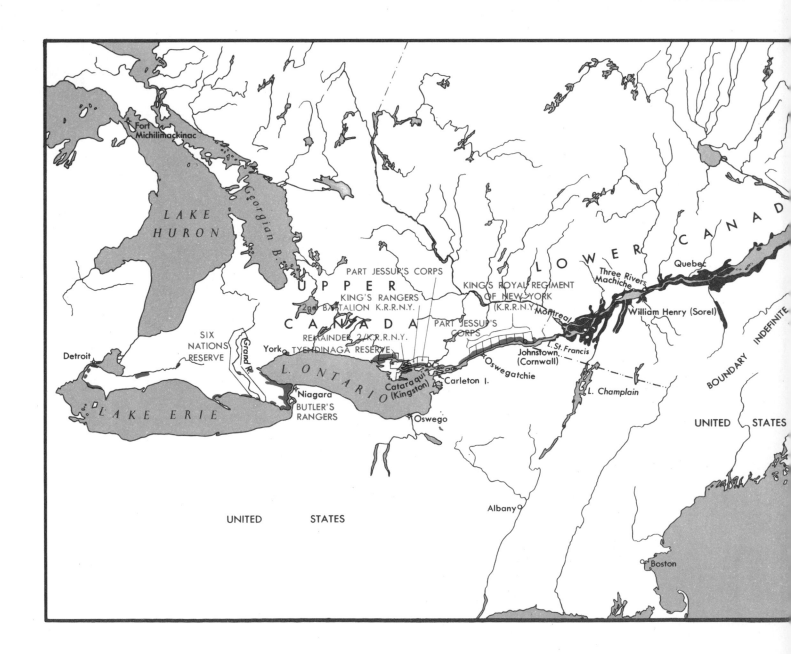

48 Military Settlements in New Brunswick

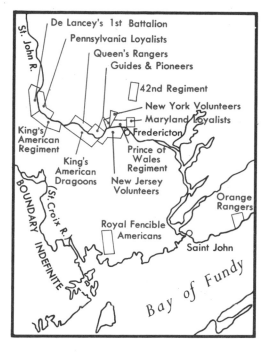

Grand River; Butler's Rangers stayed at Niagara where they had been based during the war. Other arrivals came from Detroit after the abandonment of that fort in 1796 under the terms of Jay's Treaty. In Canada, Loyalists were soon outnumbered by others moving westward with the frontier heedless of political boundaries; in the Maritimes, they remained dominant in the population for several generations.

The coming of the Loyalists coincided with and helped to cause the separation of New Brunswick and Cape Breton from Nova Scotia in 1784 and the division of Upper and Lower Canada following the Constitutional Act in 1791.

CHANGING RELATIONSHIPS, 1763–1822

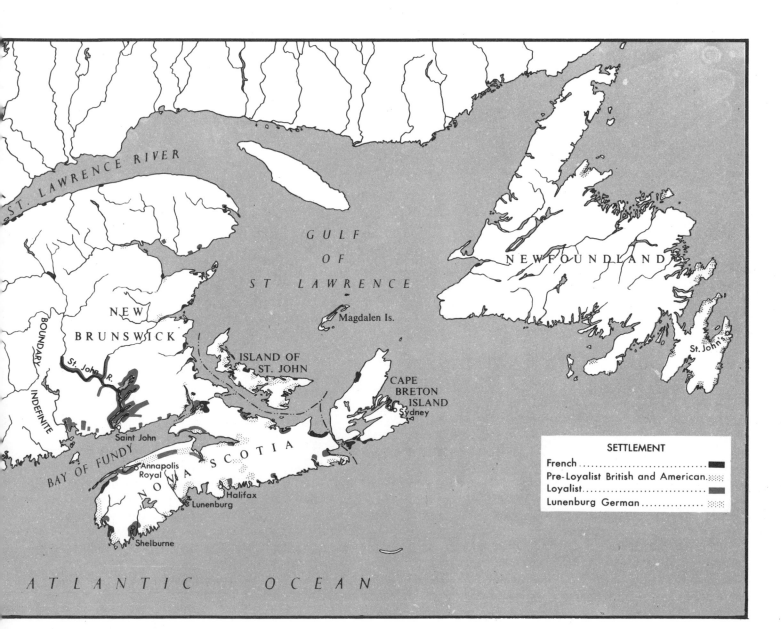

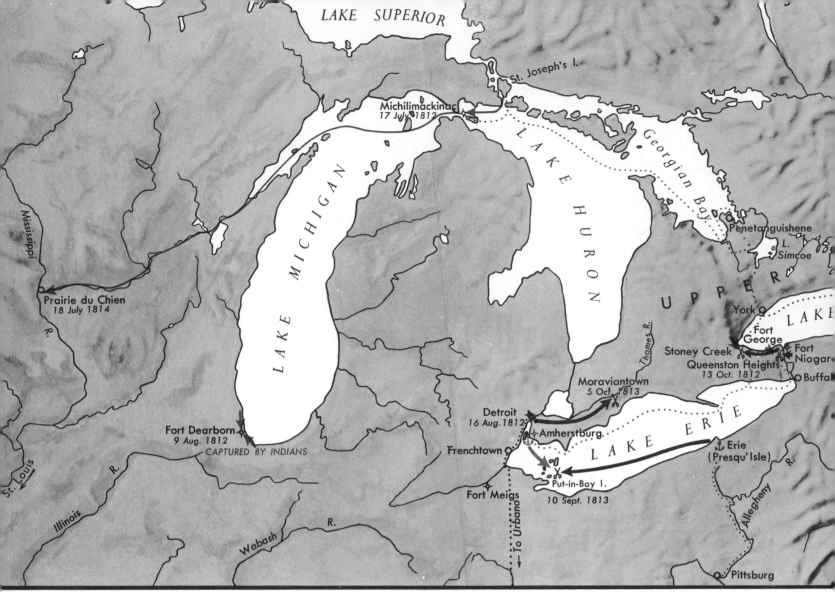

Base map copyright Canadian Aero Service Limited, Ottawa

50 The Niagara Theatre

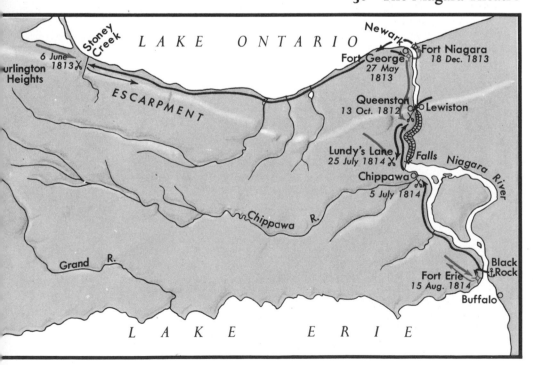

49 The War of 1812

The War of 1812, although related to the wider Napoleonic Wars and the earlier Revolutionary War and conducted partly by naval forces along the American seaboard, was primarily an American attempt to annex at least the western peninsula of Upper Canada. The main fighting, therefore, was around Niagara or farther west, and the Americans failed to concentrate on the traditional 'warpath of nations' along Lake Champlain where the capture of Montreal would have cut communications with Upper Canada and been a mortal blow. Their limited real objective also meant that the Americans fought half-heartedly at first, though with growing skill and determination as bloodshed increased, and it was possible to repel their invasion with what British troops were available aided by some militia units and Indians. Waterways being essential to communications, naval flotillas on the various lakes played a decisive role.

The main events year by year were: 1812. Shortly after the United States declared war (June 18), General Hull crossed the Detroit frontier into Canada (July 11), but retreated again when audacious British and Indian actions at Michilimackinac (July 17) and Fort Dearborn (August 9) gave

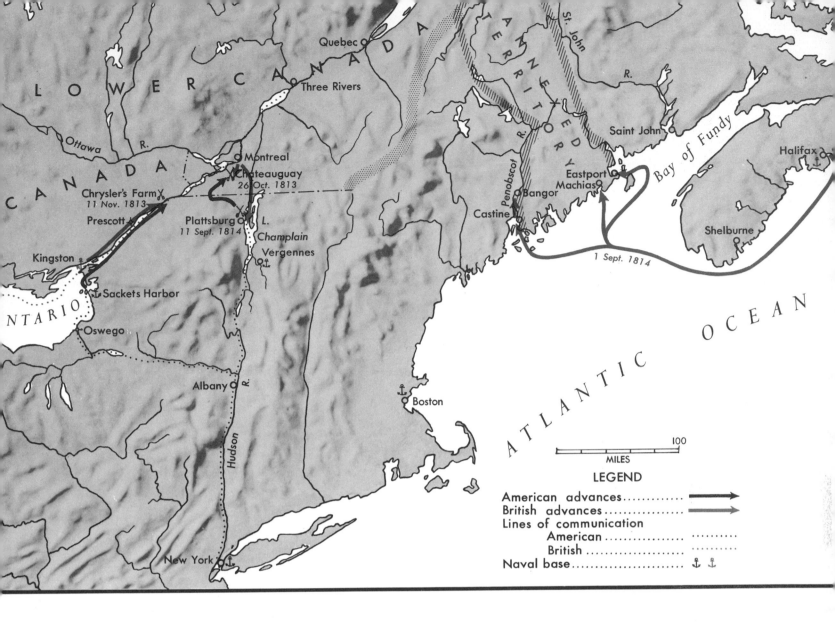

the British control of important Indian and
fur-trading territories in his rear and when
expected support from American settlers in
Upper Canada was not forthcoming. Isaac
Brock, following on his heels, captured
Detroit itself (August 16) before turning
back to bring about the defeat, at the cost
of his own life, of a more energetic American
crossing in the Niagara region at Queenston
Heights (October 13).

1813. In a second Niagara effort, the
Americans captured Fort George (May 27),
but their farther advance was halted at
Stoney Creek (June 5–6) by a daring night
attack under John Harvey, and before the
year's end Fort George had been abandoned
and the American side of the Niagara River
was being devastated by British raiders. Westward, however, a small but decisive naval
engagement at Put-in-Bay (September 10)
gave the Americans permanent command of
Lake Erie and forced a British withdrawal
towards Niagara in the course of which, in
the Battle of the Thames River near
Moraviantown (October 5), the great Indian
leader, Tecumseh, was slain. On the other
hand, in the east, a two-pronged attack on
Montreal from Lake Champlain and Lake
Ontario was effectively parried at Chateau-

guay (October 26) and Chrysler's Farm
(November 11).

1814. At Niagara, where the main fighting
now centred, the Americans captured Fort
Erie (July 3), went on to a victory at Chip-
pawa (July 5), but were turned back after a
major engagement at Lundy's Lane (July 25).
Although successful in beating off a heavy
assault on Fort Erie (August 15) they had
eventually to abandon it also (November 5)
before winter set in. Meanwhile, Napoleon's
defeat and abdication (April 11) had released
some of Wellington's veterans for Canadian
service, and Prevost, the governor-in-chief
and commander of the forces, led a powerful
invading force across the Lake Champlain
frontier (September 1). His ineptness and a
premature naval battle at Plattsburg (September 11), which gave command of Lake
Champlain to the Americans, obliged him
to retreat ignominiously. The more aggres-
sive lieutenant-governor of Nova Scotia, Sir
John Sherbrooke, was at the same time
annexing the whole district of Maine
(September 1–21) while in the far west
Britain's hold on the Indian territories had
been strengthened by the capture of Prairie
du Chien (July 18) and the successful defence
of Michilimackinac (August 4).

51 The Montreal Region

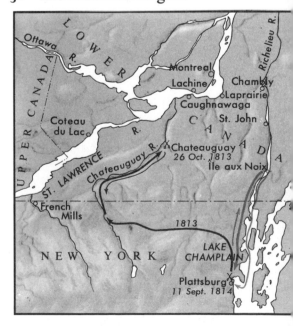

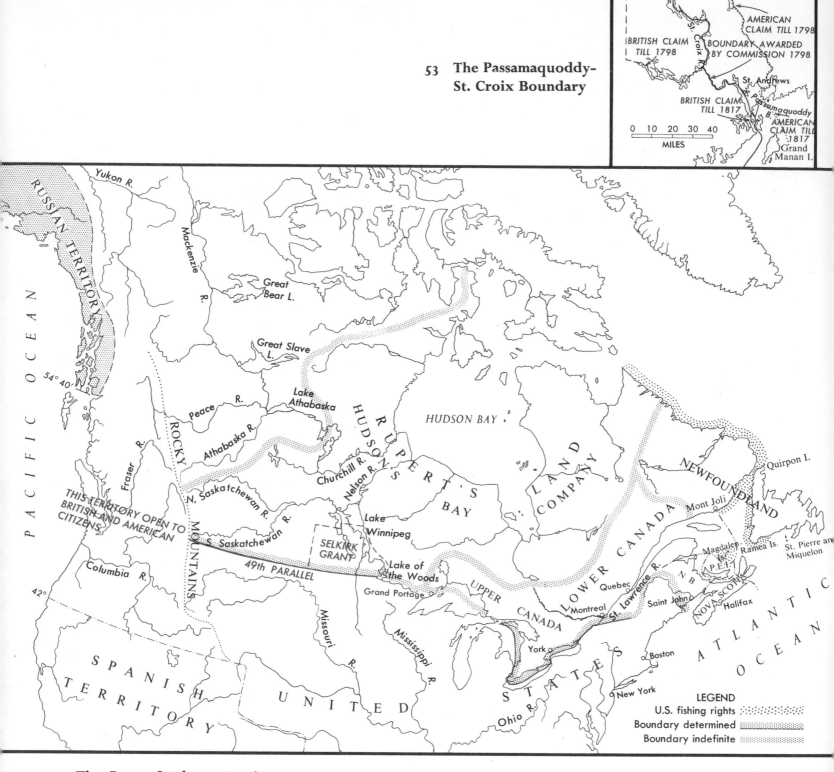

AMERICAN CLAIM TILL 1798

BRITISH CLAIM TILL 1798

BOUNDARY AWARDED BY COMMISSION 1798

St. Andrews

BRITISH CLAIM TILL 1817

Passamaquoddy B.

AMERICAN CLAIM TILL 1817

Grand Manan I.

0 10 20 30 40
MILES

52 The Peace Settlements, 1814-22

The Treaty of Ghent (December 24, 1814) dealt with none of the problems alleged as causes of war in 1812, but simply restored peace and the 1783 boundary. Its most important provisions were for several commissions to define that boundary more accurately (1) where it divided the islands of Passamaquoddy Bay, (2) in the St. Croix and Connecticut River Region, (3) from the St. Lawrence through to the waterways leading into Lake Superior, (4) through these and Lake Superior and to the north-western point of the Lake of the Woods. The first and third commissions achieved permanent settlements in reports dated November 24, 1817, and June 18, 1822, respectively. The

other two ended in disagreement and final decisions on these sections were not reached until the Webster-Ashburton Treaty of 1842 (see Map 71).

Meanwhile, notes exchanged between the British minister in Washington, Sir Charles Bagot (April 28, 1817) and the acting American secretary of state, Richard Rush (April 29, 1817) resulted in an 'Arrangement' proclaimed by President Monroe (April 28, 1818) for naval disarmament on the Lakes, each side keeping the right to only one vessel on Lake Ontario, two on the Upper Lakes, and one on Lake Champlain, none to exceed 100 tons or carry more than one 18-pounder gun. A further Convention

of Commerce between the two countries (October 20, 1818) granted Americans certain fishing rights round the Magdalen Islands, on the coasts of Newfoundland from the Ramea Islands around Cape Ray to Quirpon Island, and on Labrador (transferred back from Lower Canada to Newfoundland in 1809) from Mont Joli through the Strait of Belle Isle northward indefinitely to the Hudson's Bay Company's territories. It provided also that the British-American boundary west of the Lake of the Woods should follow the 49th parallel to the 'Stony Mountains' and that west of the mountains the territories claimed by each should be open to both for ten years.

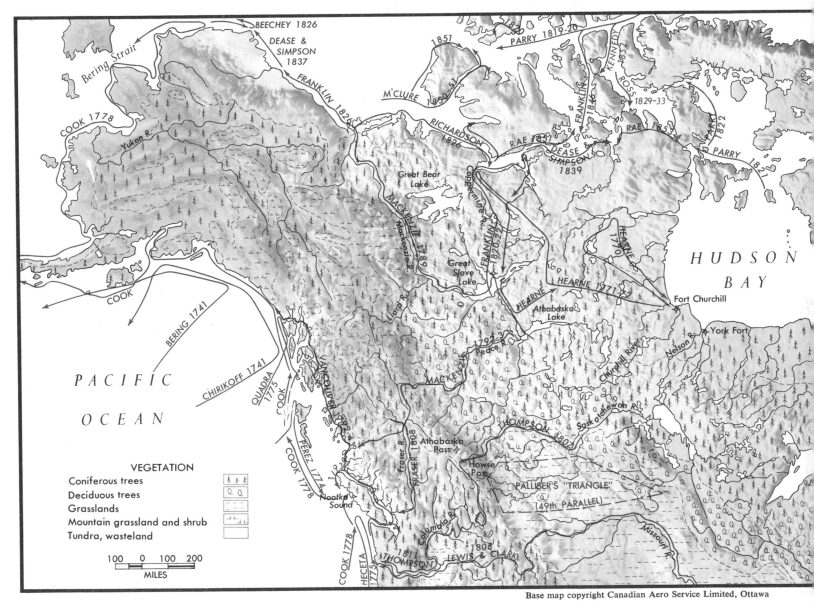

Base map copyright Canadian Aero Service Limited, Ottawa

54 The Explorers

Urged on by fur-trading and national rivalries, the exploration of the prairie, Arctic, and Pacific regions continued steadily in the century after the British conquest of Canada. The Montreal 'pedlars', banded together in the North West Company, forced the pace into newer and richer fur-trading areas and produced such great explorers as Alexander Mackenzie, Simon Fraser, and David Thompson. Hudson's Bay Company interests were furthered by Samuel Hearne and others. Governments also, well before the end of the eighteenth century, had begun to participate in exploration on grounds of national and scientific as well as commercial interest. A major role, for example, was played on the Pacific Coast by such official expeditions as those of the Russians Bering and Chirikoff, the Spaniards Pérez, Heceta, and Quadra, the Britons Cook and Vancouver, and the Americans Lewis and Clark. Similarly knowledge of the western Arctic was rounded out mainly by government-supported British expeditions including those of Parry, Franklin, Richardson, Beechey, and Rae. The Hudson's Bay Company sponsored Dease and Simpson. The many expeditions sent out in search of Franklin when he failed to return from his 1845 voyage were of special importance in adding to knowledge of the northern archipelago. Palliser and others were engaged by the British or Canadian Governments to carry out the scientific examinations of the prairies necessary to enable the homesteaders to take over from the buffalo hunters.

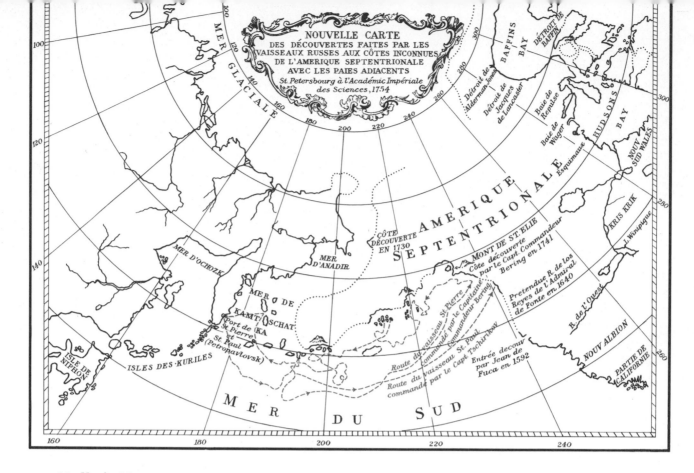

55   Muller's Map, 1754

56   Ledyard's Map, 1783

Two eighteenth-century maps, one drawn in Russia and the other in the United States, make clear the international character of Pacific Coast exploration at that time. The map prepared in St. Petersburg for the Imperial Academy of Sciences, was published in G. F. Muller's *History of Russia*. The map of Captain Cook's British expedition was published by a young American, John Ledyard, who had served with Cook.

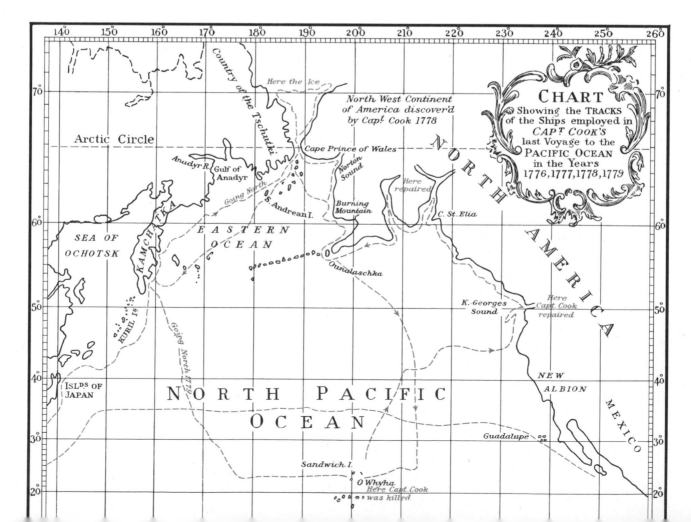

57 Oregon and British Columbia

National claims on the Pacific Coast began to be delimited when: (1) Spain abandoned all claim to the coast north of the 42nd parallel in the Treaty of Florida Blanca with the United States (February 22, 1819); and (2) Russia abandoned all claim to the coast south of the 54° 40′ parallel in treaties with the United States (April 17, 1824) and Britain (February 22, 1825). The treaty with Britain also provided that the inland boundary of Russian territory should be the first range of mountains and the 141st meridian. Meanwhile Britain and the United States had agreed in their 'Convention of Commerce' (October 20, 1818) that territories west of the mountains claimed by each should be open to the citizens of both for a ten-year period. Later renewed (October 6, 1827), this agreement broke down in the 1840's and faced with the possibility of war the two nations signed the Oregon Treaty (June 15, 1846), extending their joint boundary westward along the 49th parallel to the coast and thence through the main channel between the mainland and Vancouver Island. A later dispute as to which was the intended channel was referred in the Treaty of Washington (May 8, 1871) to the German Emperor for arbitration. His award (October 21, 1872) was in line with the American claim.

British governmental organization took shape as follows: (1) Vancouver Island was granted to the Hudson's Bay Company (January 13, 1849) on condition of establishing a colony. Its lieutenant-governor was given authority to administer the Queen Charlotte Islands (July 9, 1852) after the discovery of gold there. The colony reverted to the Crown when Hudson's Bay Company rights were revoked (May 30, 1858). (2) The Gold Rush to the Fraser Valley led to the creation of a separate crown colony of British Columbia (August 20, 1858) to which the Queen Charlotte Islands were now attached. (3) Discovery of gold in the Stikine Valley was followed by the organization of the Stikine Territory (1862) under the administration of the governor of British Columbia and its incorporation into British Columbia the following year but with somewhat altered boundaries. (4) The colonies of British Columbia and Vancouver Island were united (November 17, 1866). Meanwhile road building, largely by a party of Royal Engineers, had opened the way to the main mining centres.

THE ARCTIC, THE PLAINS, AND THE PACIFIC

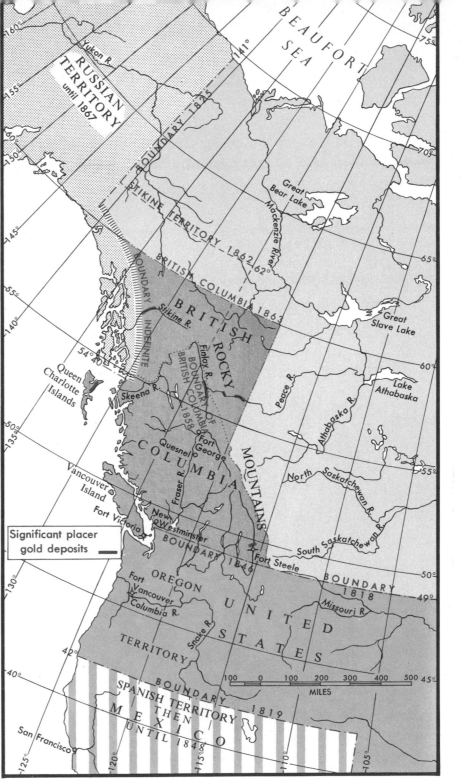

Significant placer gold deposits ▬

58 The Interior of British Columbia

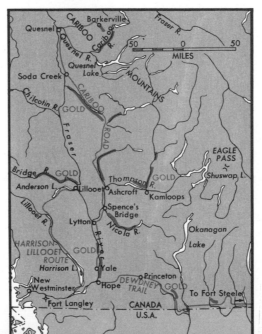

59 The San Juan Boundary Dispute

A canot de maitre

61 The Red River Settlement

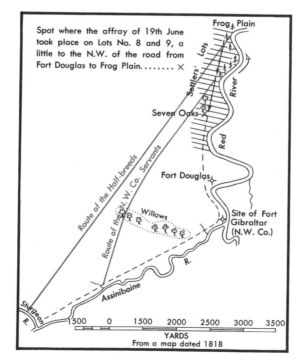

Spot where the affray of 19th June took place on Lots No. 8 and 9, a little to the N.W. of the road from Fort Douglas to Frog Plain. .... ✕

Frog Plain

Settlers' Lots

Seven Oaks

Red River

Route of the Half-breeds

Route of the N.W. Co. Servants

Fort Douglas

Willows

Site of Fort Gibraltar (N.W. Co.)

Assiniboine R.

Sturgeon R.

1500   0   1500   2000   2500   3000   3500
YARDS
From a map dated 1818

Basic in the great fur trade of the north-west were: (1) The forest belt from Lake Winnipeg to the Rockies and from the North Saskatchewan to the Arctic barrens. This was the western and widest section of the huge transcontinental northern or boreal forest, the home of the beaver and other fur-bearing animals with pelts made finer by cold winters; (2) the complex of interlocking waterways suitable for canoe transportation. The three main river systems were the Saskatchewan, draining into Lake Winnipeg and thence to Hudson Bay, the Churchill flowing directly into the Bay, and the Mackenzie into the Arctic. Two portages of key importance linking these were Frog Portage (Portage de Traite) on the most used route between the Saskatchewan and Churchill basins, and Methye Portage (Portage La Loche) between the Churchill and the Mackenzie.

Access to the region for the Montrealers of the North West Company, after they had completed their long passage to the western end of Lake Superior, was by Grand Portage until 1803. Then, because this route lay in American territory, it was abandoned in favour of one up the Kaministiquia River, at the mouth of which Fort William was built as the Nor'Westers' inland headquarters. The Hudson's Bay Company was more fortunate in having direct entry through York Fort or alternatively Fort Churchill (Fort Prince of Wales) or even Fort Albany. Rival posts at strategic places in the interior were rapidly established by both companies and at some agriculture was encouraged to supply the trappers and traders. Increasingly violent competition led to bloodshed after 1811 when the Hudson's Bay Company granted Lord Selkirk Assiniboia with its agricultural possibilities and its threat to the Nor'Westers' main communication line. Only with the amalgamation of the two companies ten years later was peace restored. The enlarged Hudson's Bay Company kept its ancient charter territory of Rupert's Land and received under terms of a twenty-one year licence from the British Government other lands to the west. These included, in addition to the Mackenzie River basin, the Rocky Mountain and Pacific Coast regions. In the latter, important for its rich trade with Canton in sea otter and other furs, the Americans had equal rights prior to the Oregon Treaty and the Hudson's Bay Company had to compete with both American and Russian fur traders.

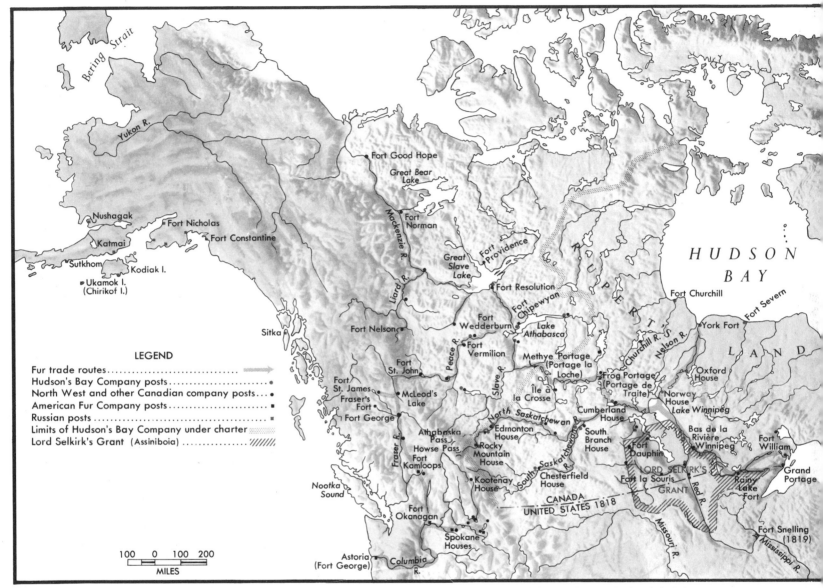

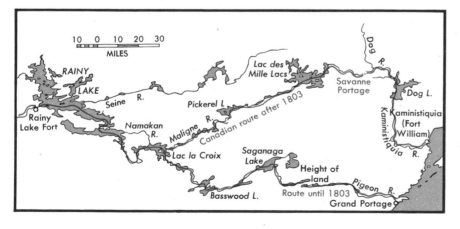

Base map copyright Canadian Aero Service Limited, Ottawa

62 The Grand Portage and Kaministiquia Routes

A York boat

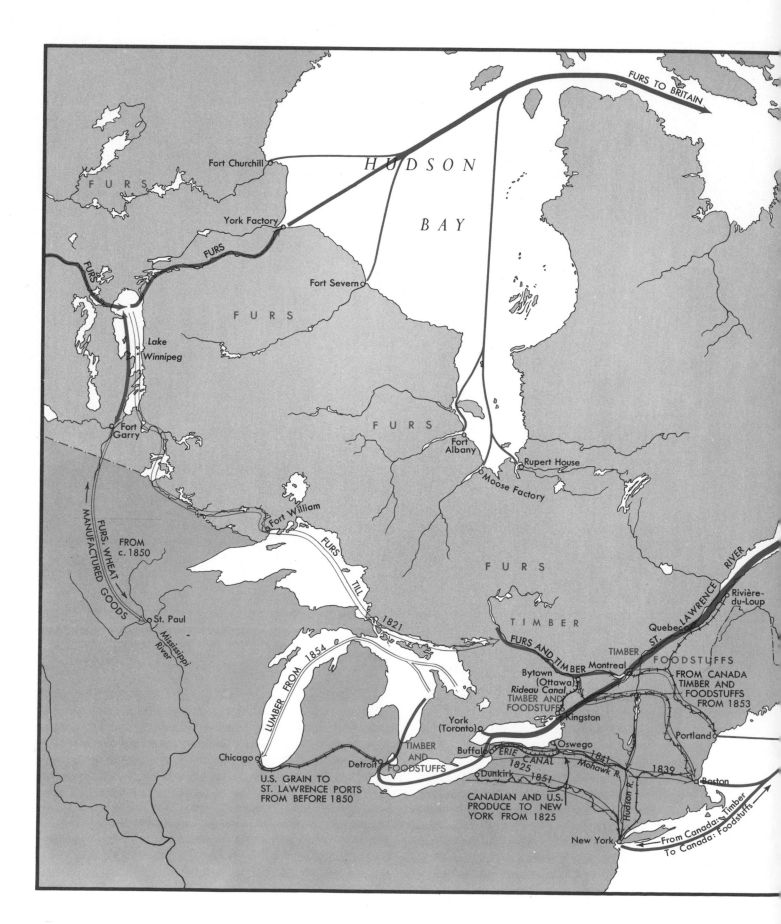

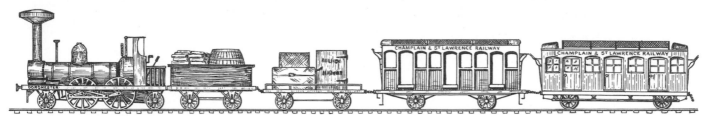

Canada's first train

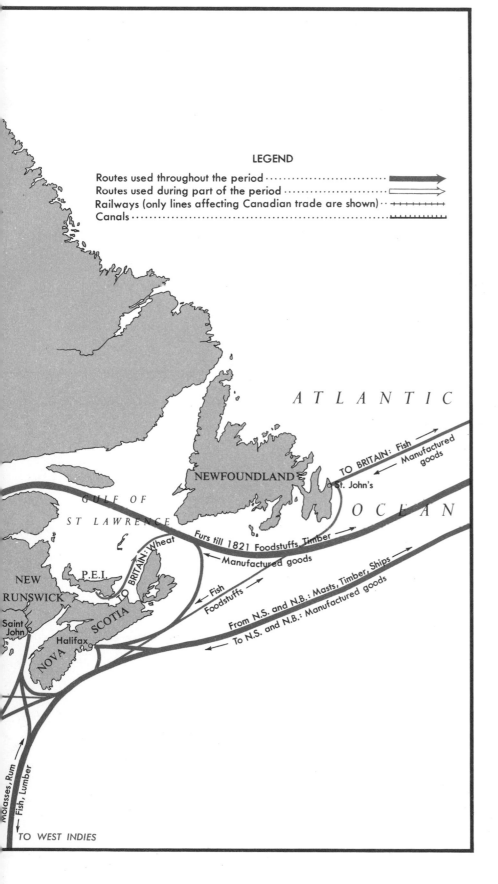

LEGEND

Routes used throughout the period ·························· ▶
Routes used during part of the period ·················· ⊳
Railways (only lines affecting Canadian trade are shown) ·· +++++++++
Canals ·· ⊞⊞⊞⊞⊞⊞⊞

ATLANTIC

NEWFOUNDLAND

St. John's

TO BRITAIN: Fish →
← Manufactured goods

OCEAN

GULF OF
ST LAWRENCE

Furs till 1821 Foodstuffs, Timber →
← Manufactured goods

TO BRITAIN: Wheat

P.E.I.

NEW
BRUNSWICK

Fish
Foodstuffs →

← Fish
Foodstuffs

From N.S. and N.B.: Masts, Timber, Ships →
← To N.S. and N.B.: Manufactured goods

Saint
John

NOVA SCOTIA

Halifax

Molasses, Rum ↑
Fish, Lumber ↑
↑ TO WEST INDIES

63   The Commercial Empire of the St. Lawrence

The British North American Provinces (including Newfoundland) grew in population from not quite half a million early in the nineteenth century to about three and a half million in 1861, the time of the last census in most of them before Confederation. Economic changes were correspondingly great. Early dependence on the fur trade and the fisheries was replaced by greater emphasis on the export of timber and grain and by the gradual development of secondary industries such as lumber and flour milling and shipbuilding. The construction of roads, canals, and railways became essential and proceeded apace, although less rapidly than in the United States. The relationship of the St. Lawrence to its old commercial rivals, Hudson Bay and the Hudson River, changed too. It lost to Hudson Bay the whole fur trade of the north-west after the amalgamation of the North West and the Hudson's Bay Companies in 1821. Although its total trade continued to grow, with growing exports of timber and grain, the St. Lawrence fell gradually further behind the Hudson River of which the natural advantages were enhanced by the opening of the Erie Canal in 1825 and by rapidly extending railways into the interior.

THE CANADAS, 1791–1867

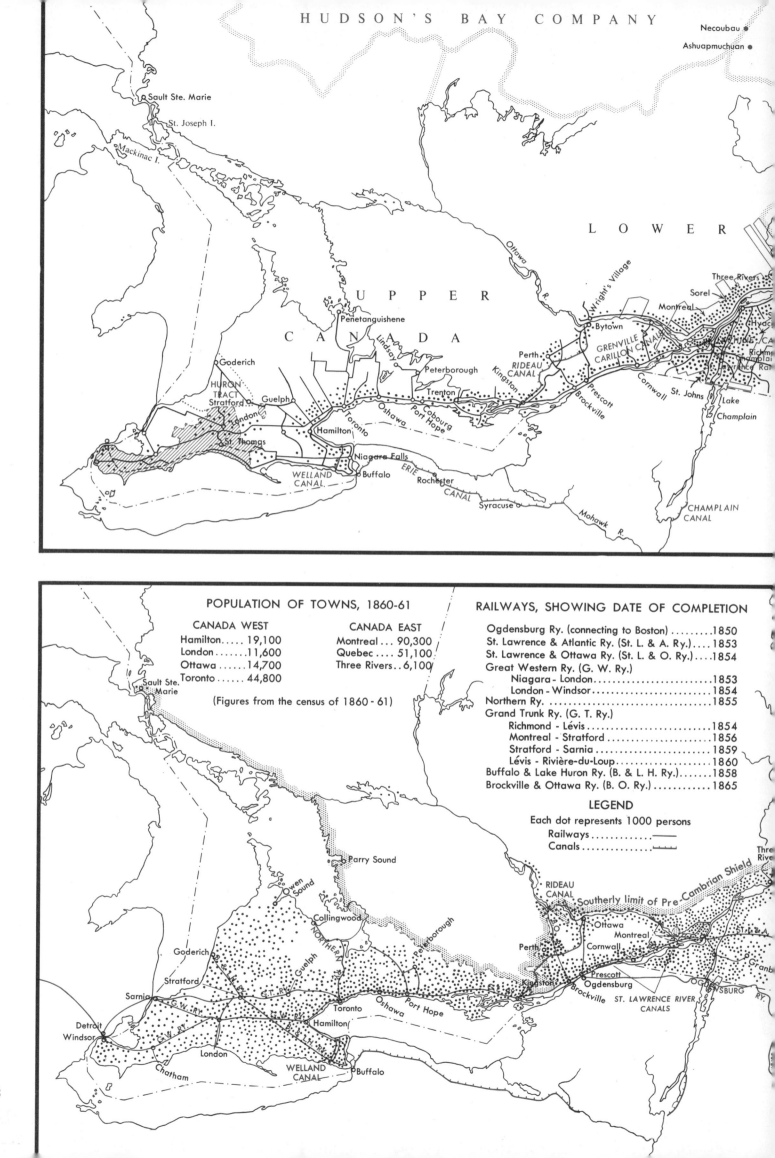

Necoubau
Ashuapmuchuan

L O W E R

U P P E R

C A N A D A

Sault Ste. Marie
St. Joseph I.
Mackinac I.

Penetanguishene

Ottawa R.

Wright's Village

Three Rivers
Sorel
Montreal

Bytown

GRENVILLE
CARILLON CANAL

Goderich

Lindsay

Perth
Peterborough
RIDEAU
CANAL
Kingston

Richmond
Lawrence Rat

HURON
TRACT
Stratford
Guelph

Trenton
Cobourg
Port Hope
Toronto
Oshawa

Prescott
Brockville
Cornwall
St. Johns

Lake
Champlain

London
St. Thomas
Hamilton

Niagara Falls
WELLAND
CANAL
Buffalo
Rochester
Syracuse

ERIE
CANAL
Mohawk R.

CHAMPLAIN
CANAL

POPULATION OF TOWNS, 1860-61

CANADA WEST
Hamilton..... 19,100
London.......11,600
Ottawa 14,700
Toronto 44,800

CANADA EAST
Montreal ... 90,300
Quebec 51,100
Three Rivers.. 6,100

(Figures from the census of 1860 - 61)

RAILWAYS, SHOWING DATE OF COMPLETION

Ogdensburg Ry. (connecting to Boston) 1850
St. Lawrence & Atlantic Ry. (St. L. & A. Ry.)....1853
St. Lawrence & Ottawa Ry. (St. L. & O. Ry.)....1854
Great Western Ry. (G. W. Ry.)
    Niagara - London...........................1853
    London - Windsor..........................1854
Northern Ry. 1855
Grand Trunk Ry. (G. T. Ry.)
    Richmond - Lévis 1854
    Montreal - Stratford 1856
    Stratford - Sarnia 1859
    Lévis - Rivière-du-Loup...................1860
Buffalo & Lake Huron Ry. (B. & L. H. Ry.).......1858
Brockville & Ottawa Ry. (B. O. Ry.) 1865

LEGEND
Each dot represents 1000 persons
Railways ...._____
Canals ....├┴┴┴┤

Sault Ste.
Marie

Parry Sound

Owen
Sound

Collingwood

RIDEAU
CANAL

Southerly limit of Pre-Cambrian Shield

Three
Rivers

Goderich

NORTHERN

Peterborough

Ottawa
Montreal

Perth
Cornwall

ST. L. & A.

Granb

Stratford
Guelph

Port Hope

Kingston
Prescott
Ogdensburg
Brockville

OGDENSBURG
RY.

Sarnia
G.T. RY.

Toronto
Oshawa

ST. LAWRENCE RIVER
CANALS

Detroit
Windsor
G.W. RY.

G.W. RY.

Hamilton

B. & L. H. RY.

London

Chatham

WELLAND
CANAL
Buffalo

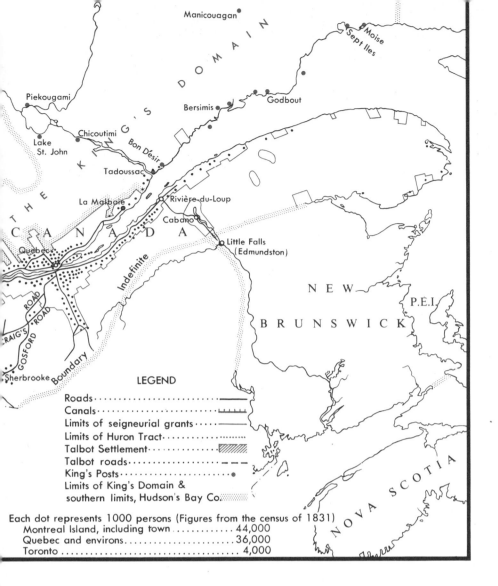

LEGEND

Roads ....
Canals ....
Limits of seigneurial grants .....
Limits of Huron Tract ....
Talbot Settlement ....
Talbot roads ....
King's Posts ....
Limits of King's Domain &
   southern limits, Hudson's Bay Co.

Each dot represents 1000 persons (Figures from the census of 1831)
Montreal Island, including town 44,000
Quebec and environs 36,000
Toronto 4,000

64 Settlement and Communications to 1840

Upper Canada attracted immigration after it became a separate province in 1791 and newcomers soon greatly outnumbered the original Loyalists. Before the War of 1812 most were Americans, but the influx afterwards, which included some disbanded troops, was mainly from the British Isles. Lower Canada with its outdated seigneuries, not abolished until 1854, progressed more slowly except in the freehold Eastern Townships.

Settlement was assisted to some extent by governments but also by land companies, emigration societies, and private individuals such as Thomas Talbot. It was handicapped at first by the clergy- and crown-reserves policy of the British Government and by corruption and inefficiency in land administration.

Early improvements in communications, so vital to settlement, took the form of road and canal building and after 1809 the rapid growth of steamship services. In the 1830's railroads began to be projected but prior to the Act of Union of 1840 only the sixteen-mile Champlain and St. Lawrence line had actually come into operation. The next decades saw the completion and improvement of the canal systems and, in particular, quite extensive railway building totalling almost 2,000 miles by 1860.

With these changes the old fur trade, except at the King's Posts (leased by the Hudson's Bay Company, 1842–59), gave way to agriculture, lumbering, shipbuilding, etc.

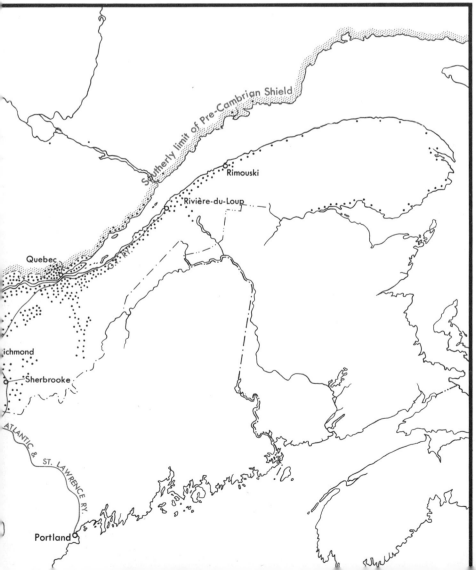

65 Settlement and Communications, 1841–67

66 A Township with 'Chequer Board' Reserves

The township was the unit of settlement during the British period as the seigneury had been during the French. The typical township was ten miles square or, if on navigable water, twelve miles in depth with a nine-mile water frontage. Modifications due to local circumstances were very frequent, however. The Constitutional Act of 1791 provided that lands 'equal in value to the Seventh Part' of grants made since the beginning of British rule, and subsequently of all future grants, should be reserved in both Upper and Lower Canada for use of the Protestant clergy, and Colonial Office instructions reserved another seventh for the Crown. The usual 'chequer board' pattern of these reserves scattered them evenly throughout each township. Being held for later and more profitable sale they helped impede early settlement. The crown reserves in Upper Canada (1,384,413 acres) together with the Huron Tract (1,000,000 acres) were eventually disposed of to the Canada Company in 1825. A similar arrangement regarding the crown reserves in Lower Canada (251,336 acres) and other unsurveyed land (596,325 acres) was made in 1834 with the British American Land Company. Gradual sale of the clergy reserves was authorized in 1827 and the final secularization of those remaining took place in 1854.

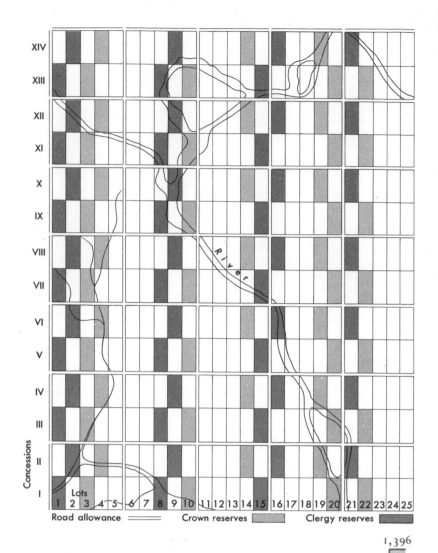

Road allowance ———   Crown reserves   Clergy reserves

67 The Growth of Population

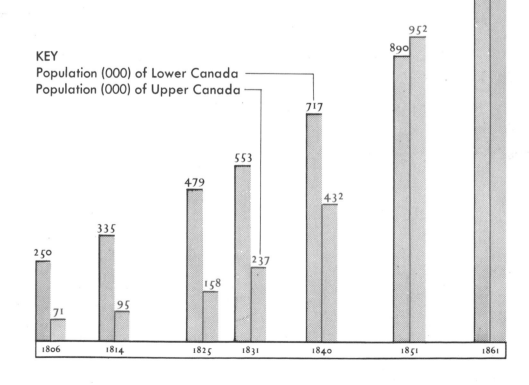

KEY
Population (000) of Lower Canada ———
Population (000) of Upper Canada ———

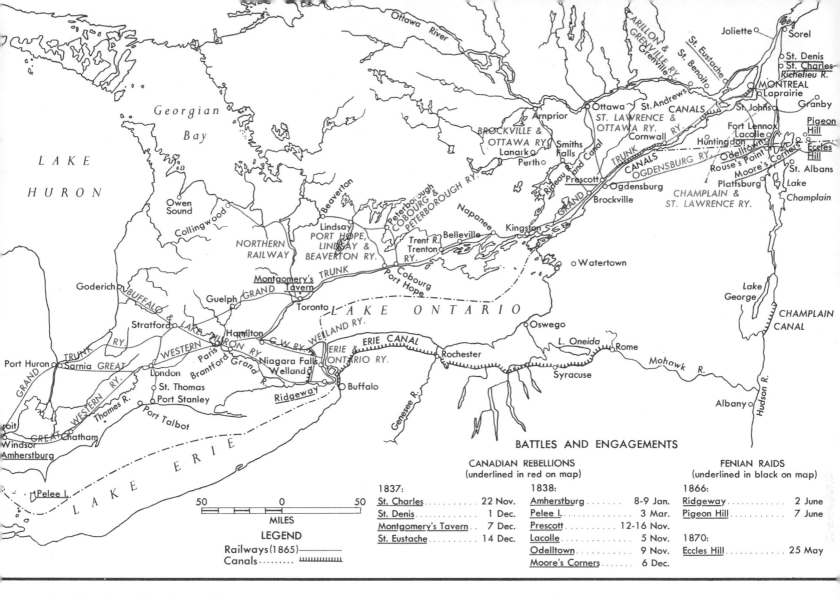

BATTLES AND ENGAGEMENTS

CANADIAN REBELLIONS (underlined in red on map)				FENIAN RAIDS (underlined in black on map)	
1837:		**1838:**		**1866:**	
St. Charles	22 Nov.	Amherstburg	8-9 Jan.	Ridgeway	2 June
St. Denis	1 Dec.	Pelee I.	3 Mar.	Pigeon Hill	7 June
Montgomery's Tavern	7 Dec.	Prescott	12-16 Nov.		
St. Eustache	14 Dec.	Lacolle	5 Nov.	**1870:**	
		Odelltown	9 Nov.	Eccles Hill	25 May
		Moore's Corners	6 Dec.		

LEGEND

Railways (1865) ———
Canals .... ⊔⊔⊔⊔⊔⊔

68 The Canadian Rebellions, 1837–8

Political and other grievances, made more bitter in Lower Canada by racial division, led to armed violence beginning with rioting in Montreal in November, 1837. During the next month or so there were serious clashes, the chief centres of disaffection being the Richelieu parishes and the Lake of Two Mountains area. After an initial check at St. Denis, regular troops and volunteers suppressed the disturbances, the final and most bloody encounter being at St. Eustache. In Upper Canada a farcical encounter between government supporters and rebels on Toronto's Yonge Street was followed by hasty flight on both sides. The following day (December 7) a city militia force dispersed the rebels at Montgomery's Tavern. Troubles were prolonged for a few months by rebels who escaped to the United States and with the aid of quite numerous American sympathizers undertook a variety of futile skirmishes across the border including a serious raid at Prescott which coincided with a brief second rebellion in Lower Canada.

The Fenian Raids, 1866–71

The Fenian Brotherhood, organized in Ireland and among Irish Americans to win Ireland's independence from Britain, took advantage of the general restlessness in the United States and hostility towards Britain following the American Civil War to make several raids on Canada. A half-hearted attempt on New Brunswick's Campobello Island was followed by a much more serious effort under John O'Neill who led 1,500 Fenians across the Niagara River on May 31, 1866, and won a victory over a Canadian force at Ridgeway before withdrawing. Simultaneously there was some plundering on the border east of Lake Champlain and a minor raid was repulsed near Huntingdon. Despite many alarms, the only other major raid was in May, 1870, when a force raised by O'Neill was met by resolute Canadians at Eccles Hill and driven back across the border. An attempt on Manitoba in 1871 was broken up by American troops.

THE CANADAS, 1791–1867

The sea was fundamental to the economy of the Atlantic Colonies. It supplied them with their valuable inshore and bank fisheries and with access to the markets of Europe and the West Indies. Although all four colonies had much in common, each acquired distinctive characteristics. Newfoundland depended almost entirely on the cod fisheries. Nova Scotia had in addition a substantial

shipbuilding and shipping industry and some coal mining and agriculture. New Brunswick rivalled Nova Scotia in shipbuilding and shipping, exported a large amount of squared timber to Britain and miscellaneous lumber and staves to the West Indies, and carried on some fishing and agriculture. Agriculture was Prince Edward Island's main resource.

Settlement throughout the region was along the coast or up main river valleys. It was encouraged by the cheap though extremely hazardous and uncomfortable passages available to immigrants in returning timber ships. Even so it took place more slowly than in the Canadas.

Roads and stage coaches soon supplemented river and coastal shipping. This

69   A Maritime Economy

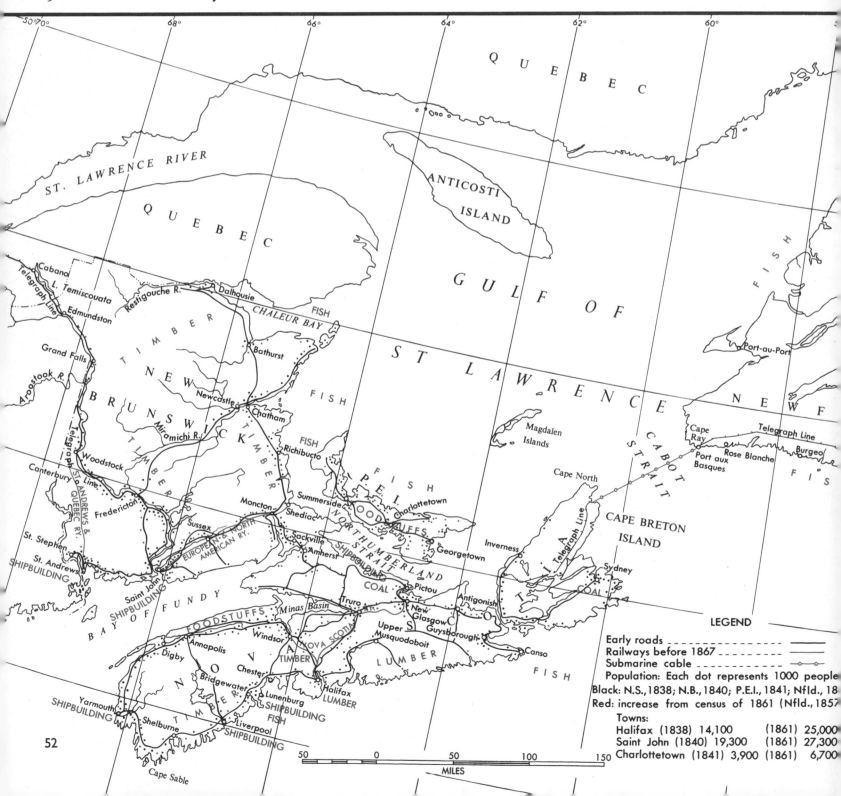

latter was greatly improved when steamships began to be introduced in the 1820's. The first regular trans-Atlantic steamship service was inaugurated by Samuel Cunard of Halifax in 1840. Railway construction by 1866 amounted to 218 miles in New Brunswick and 147 miles in Nova Scotia.

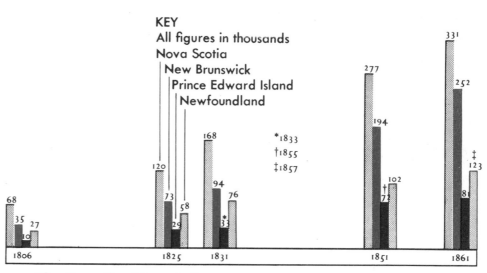

KEY
All figures in thousands
Nova Scotia
New Brunswick
Prince Edward Island
Newfoundland

*1833
†1855
‡1857

70   The Growth of Population

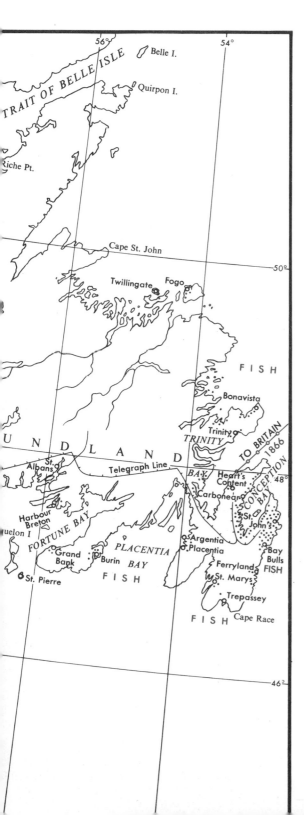

71   The Webster-Ashburton Boundary Settlement, 1842

Badly defined in the Treaty of Paris (1783) and despite further efforts under the terms of Jay's Treaty (1794) and the Treaty of Ghent (1814), the American border with New Brunswick and Canada remained undetermined when lumbermen from both sides began to enter the region in the 1820's. An American threat in 1828, firmly resisted by the New Brunswick authorities, led to a request for arbitration by the King of the Netherlands, but his Award (1831) was rejected by the United States. More serious local disturbances in 1839 followed by warlike threats and preparations by the governments concerned—the so-called Aroostook or 'Pork and Beans' War—made clear the need for a final settlement. This was achieved in the Webster-Ashburton Treaty (1842) which, although it left a wedge of Maine projecting between New Brunswick and Canada, kept intact the vital communication route from Fredericton to Quebec via Lake Temiscouata and was more favourable to Britain than the Award of 1831 had been.

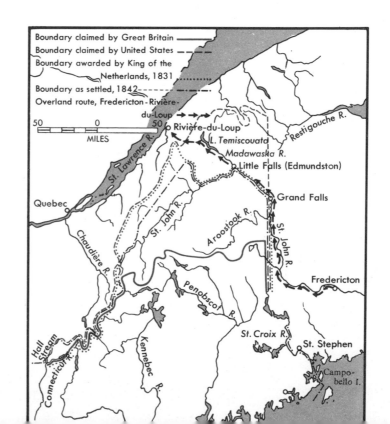

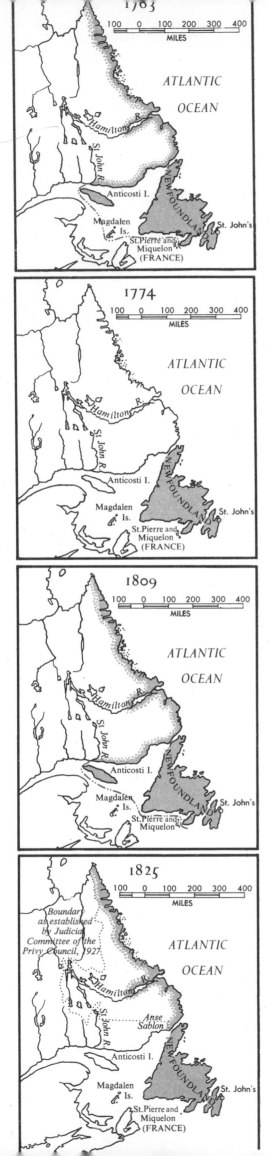

Newfoundland and Labrador

73 in 1763
74 in 1774
75 in 1809
76 in 1825

The fisheries constituted the key to Newfoundland's evolution in the century before 1867. They account for the fact that when France was obliged to give up all other Newfoundland claims in the Treaty of Utrecht (1713) she insisted on keeping fishing rights along what came to be known as the 'French Shore'. These rights were modified slightly in the Treaty of Versailles (1783), were lost during the French Revolutionary and Napoleonic Wars, and were renewed in the Treaty of Paris (1815). They denied British subjects effective use of a large part of Newfoundland's coastline until finally abrogated in 1904. The United States managed to obtain similar, but less extensive, rights along part of the coast in the Convention of Commerce (1818) and round all of it in the Reciprocity Treaty (1854–65).

Meanwhile Labrador and some adjacent islands passed back and forth several times between Newfoundland and Canada in response to pressure from rival fishing and other interests. Anticosti, the Magdalen Islands, and Labrador from the St. John River to Hudson Strait were first transferred from the newly acquired Canada to Newfoundland by Royal Proclamation (1763) and then returned to Canada by the Quebec Act (1774). Newfoundland got back all but the Magdalen Islands in the first Labrador Act (1809) but again lost Anticosti and the coast of Labrador as far east as Anse Sablon in the second Labrador Act (1825). Not until a decision by the Judicial Committee of the Privy Council in 1927 was the Labrador-Quebec boundary finally determined.

72 Newfoundland Fisheries

The British North America Act of March 29, 1867, provided for the confederation of the colonies of Canada (simultaneously to be divided into Ontario and Quebec), New Brunswick, and Nova Scotia, and for their being linked by an intercolonial railway. The Dominion of Canada came into existence accordingly on July 1, 1867, and the railway was formally opened on July 1, 1876. Meanwhile on July 15, 1870, after lengthy negotiations with the Hudson's Bay Company and the British Government, and after further delays due to the Red River Insurrection, the Hudson's Bay and Northwest Territories were transferred to Canada, part becoming the Province of Manitoba and the rest being placed under territorial government. A year later, on July 20, 1871, British Columbia entered Confederation on terms that included, among other things, the building of a transcontinental railway line.

78 Prince Edward Island's Proprietors

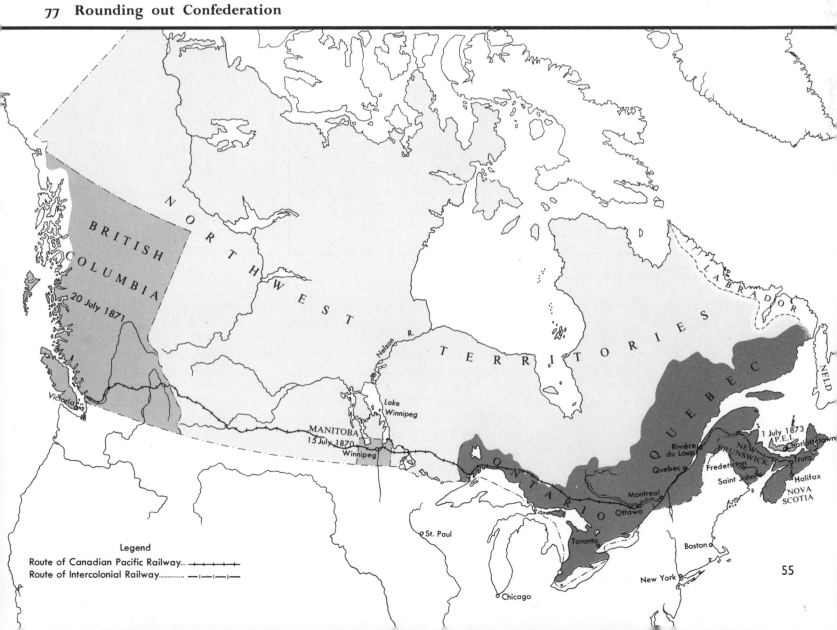

The Canadian Pacific Railway built to meet this undertaking was completed November 7, 1885. Prince Edward Island joined Canada on July 1, 1873, on being promised the maintenance of continuous communications with the mainland, the taking over and completion of her railway, and aid in buying out her proprietors. These latter, many of them absentees, were the owners of the 67 lots into which the Island had been divided in 1767.

77 Rounding out Confederation

Legend

Route of Canadian Pacific Railway........ +++++++
Route of Intercolonial Railway............. —·—·—·—

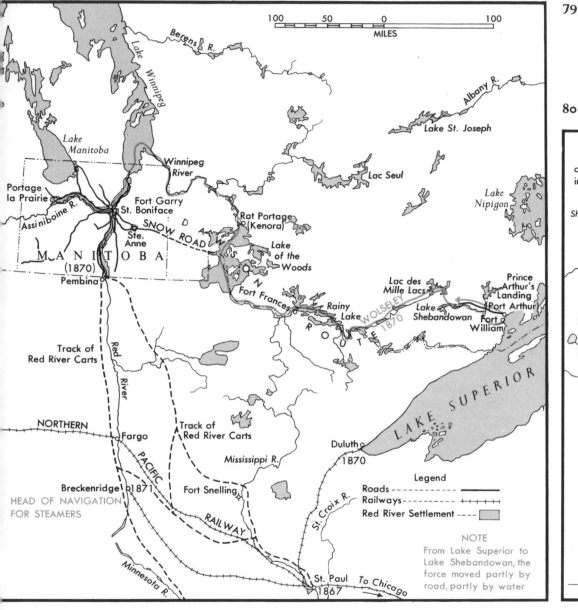

79 The Creation of Manitoba

80 Colonel Dennis' Land Survey

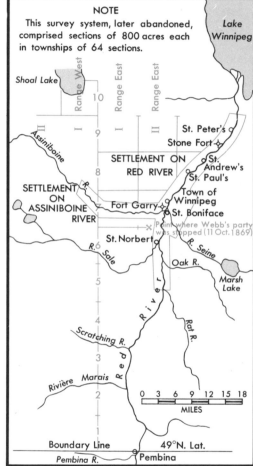

NOTE

This survey system, later abandoned, comprised sections of 800 acres each in townships of 64 sections.

The Red River Insurrection, 1869–70

The opening of the West, with its repercussions on the rest of Canada as well, was among the most important features of Canadian history between Confederation and the First World War. The beginning was unfortunate. The Red River Insurrection occurred at the outset when negotiations for the transfer to Canada of the Hudson's Bay and Northwest Territories failed to take into sufficient account the interests and anxieties of their inhabitants. The great majority of these, apart from the scattered Indian tribes, lived in the Red River Settlement and most were semi-nomadic half-breeds, mainly French-speaking and Roman Catholic. The half-breeds' fears that an influx of settlers from Canada (probably English and Protestant) would follow the transfer were strengthened by two preliminary Canadian actions, the commencement in 1868 of a road forming the most westerly portion of the combined road and river route between Port Arthur and Fort Garry recommended in 1858 by S. J. Dawson, and the general land survey undertaken in the summer of 1869 by a party under Colonel J. S. Dennis. Dennis' survey, although based on the American system of square townships, was accompanied by a careful promise to respect claims to existing strip farms running back from the Red and Assiniboine Rivers. That it provoked the half-breeds to physical resistance was because it seemed an assertion of Canadian authority over-riding any right of the inhabitants even to consultation. Full-scale insurrection followed with Louis Riel assuming the leadership.

Eventually after Canadian negotiations with Riel's provisional government had resulted in the passage of the Manitoba Act (May 12, 1870), the 14,340 square mile province of Manitoba and the Northwest Territories became part of Canada (July 15, 1870). To ensure against further disorders and to

81 Indian Treaties

satisfy public opinion in Ontario aroused by Riel's execution of Thomas Scott, a military expedition under Colonel G. J. Wolseley was sent to Fort Garry, arriving August 24, 1870.

The advance of settlement into the plains and later the north-west led to the negotiation of treaties in which the Indians agreed to surrender their general claims to the land in return for reservations and certain gifts and annuities. The bloodshed common along the American frontier was almost entirely avoided by means of this policy and as a result also of certain other factors, notably the tradition of law and order established by the Hudson's Bay Company and maintained by the North-west Mounted Police, and the existence in Canada of a considerable half-breed population to serve as intermediaries between white and Indian.

OPENING THE WEST AND NORTH

A Gatling gun

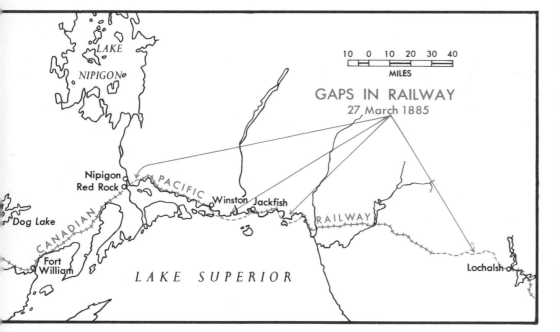

GAPS IN RAILWAY
27 March 1885

10 0 10 20 30 40
MILES

LAKE SUPERIOR

LAKE NIPIGON

Dog Lake

Nipigon
Red Rock

Winston Jackfish

PACIFIC

CANADIAN

RAILWAY

Fort William

Lochalsh

83   Gaps in the C.P.R.

82   The North-west Insurrection, 1885

For a variety of reasons, some resulting from errors or indifference on the part of the Government at Ottawa, the white settlers, half-breeds, and Indians of Canada's Northwest Territories were all becoming increasingly restless and discontented in the early 1880's. In 1884, at their invitation, Louis Riel returned from exile in the United States and on March 19, 1885, in spite of strong opposition from the Roman Catholic clergy, he proclaimed a provisional government at Batoche, the centre of French half-breed settlement in the Saskatchewan District. Not prepared to go to such an extreme, the settlers and English half-breeds remained aloof as did the Indians of the great Blackfoot Confederacy and most of the Crees, except for bands led by Poundmaker and Big Bear. Nevertheless, when fighting began near Duck Lake on March 26, a mounted police and militia force was defeated and soon the whole area was in French half-breed or Indian hands except for weakly held positions at Prince Albert, Battleford, and Fort Saskatchewan.

Rapid suppression of the uprising before it could become widespread or well organized was made possible by the use of the telegraph to send immediate word to Ottawa and use of the Canadian Pacific Railway, completed except for a few gaps north of Lake Superior, to send troops (militia and some units of the new Permanent Force) to the scene. Two Gatling machine-guns and two small steamers on the South Saskatchewan were innovations to prairie warfare.

The advance against the rebels was made by three columns. The largest led by General Middleton moved cautiously north from Fort Qu'Appelle and after an indecisive encounter at Fish Creek (April 24), took Batoche (May 12) and captured Riel (May 15). Lieutenant-Colonel Otter pushed ahead rapidly from Swift Current and relieved civilians held for a month at the mercy of the Indians at Battleford (April 25), but was checked by Poundmaker in a skirmish at Cut Knife Hill (May 2). Major-General Strange reached Edmonton from Calgary and moved down the North Saskatchewan until stopped by Big Bear at Frenchman's Butte (May 28). Meanwhile Middleton had advanced to Battleford in mopping-up operations and accepted Poundmaker's surrender (May 26). He went on to join Strange near Fort Pitt and the rebellion ended when Big Bear gave himself up (July 2).

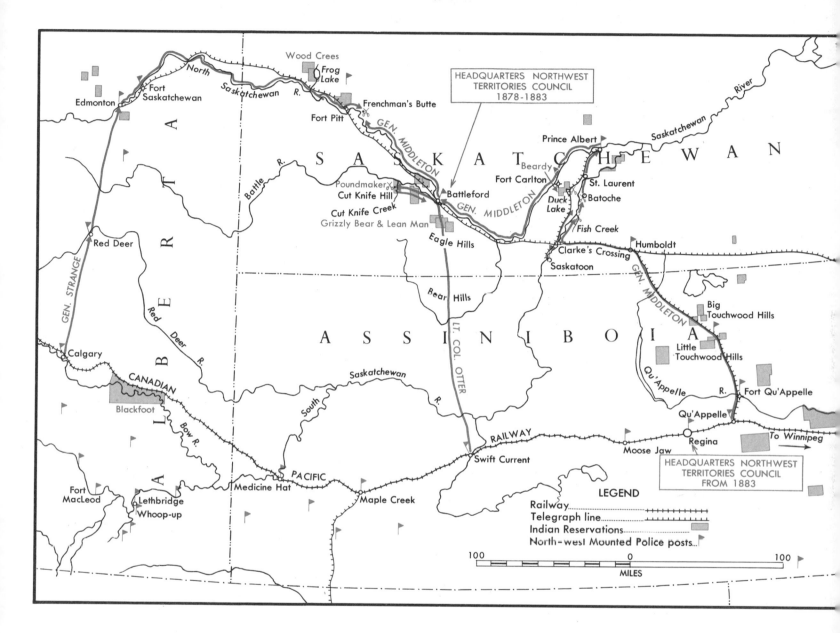

Wood Crees
Frog
Lake
Frenchman's Butte
North *Saskatchewan* R.
Edmonton
Fort Saskatchewan
Fort Pitt

HEADQUARTERS NORTHWEST
TERRITORIES COUNCIL
1878-1883

Saskatchewan River
Prince Albert

Battle R.
S A S K A T C H E W A N
GEN. MIDDLETON
Beardy
Fort Carlton
St. Laurent
Poundmaker X
Cut Knife Hill
Cut Knife Creek
Grizzly Bear & Lean Man
Battleford
GEN. MIDDLETON
Duck
Lake
Batoche
Fish Creek
Eagle Hills
Clarke's Crossing
Humboldt
Saskatoon
GEN. MIDDLETON

A L B E R T A

Red Deer
GEN. STRANGE

Bear Hills

A S S I N I B O I A

Big
Touchwood Hills
Little
Touchwood Hills

Red *Deer* R.

Calgary

Saskatchewan R.
LT. COL. OTTER

Qu'Appelle R.
Fort Qu'Appelle

CANADIAN
Blackfoot
South *Saskatchewan* R.
Bow R.

Qu'Appelle

To Winnipeg

RAILWAY
Swift Current
Moose Jaw
Regina

HEADQUARTERS NORTHWEST
TERRITORIES COUNCIL
FROM 1883

Fort
MacLeod
Lethbridge
Whoop-up
Medicine Hat
PACIFIC
Maple Creek

LEGEND
Railway...................................
Telegraph line........................
Indian Reservations..............
North-west Mounted Police posts...

100   0   100
MILES

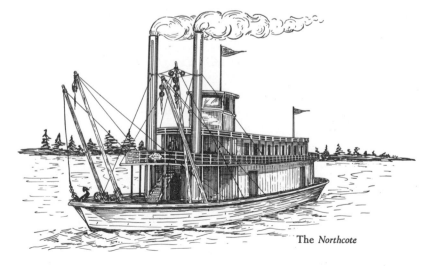

The *Northcote*

OPENING THE WEST AND NORTH

59

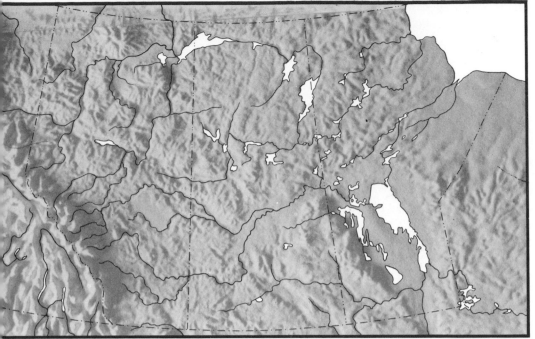

84   Relief

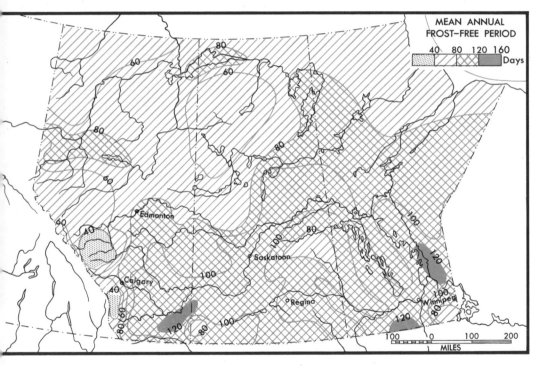

85   Mean Annual Frost-free Period

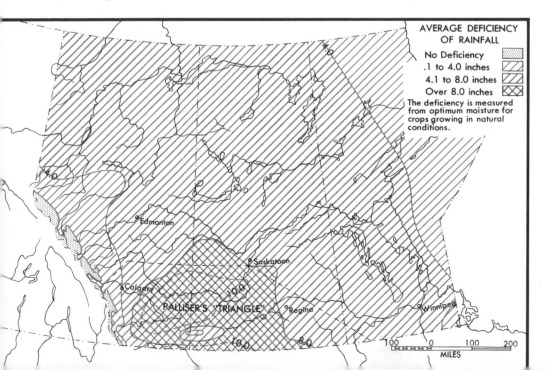

Physical Conditions in the Prairie Region

The suitability of the prairie region for agricultural settlement, long denied by Hudson's Bay Company officials, was investigated late in the 1850's by Captain John Palliser on behalf of the British Government and by S. J. Dawson and Professor H. Y. Hind for Canada. The findings of the Canadians at least, were quite optimistic with regard to a fertile belt between the south-western arid 'triangle', so called by Palliser, and the northern forests. As time went on factual knowledge of the region's physical features and their relationship to settlement was expanded by others, notably the somewhat over-enthusiastic John Macoun, a botanist who made his observations in the 1870's during preliminary surveys for the Canadian Pacific Railway.

Basic determinants of settlements have in fact been: (1) relief and topography; (2) the number of frost-free days normally to be expected between the last killing frost of spring and the first of fall; (3) aridity, a complex factor depending mainly on the amount of rainfall, especially during the growing season, but modified by other conditions such as excessive heat and evaporation; (4) the nature of the various soils, which in turn is partly dependent on the type of original vegetation—for example, the very rich dark-brown soils of the Park Belt are in the region distinguished by tall prairie grass and an annual rainfall of at least fifteen inches.

Early adverse judgements of Hudson's Bay Company officials had not been simply the result of the fur trader's natural prejudice against settlement. They proved indeed to be sounder in many respects during the nineteenth century than Canadian optimism, the actual progress of settlement being very slow. It could be accelerated only after railway and other transportation facilities had been laboriously provided, dry farming and improved agricultural machinery had been developed, and quick-maturing strains of wheat had been introduced—Red Fife by 1900, Marquis by 1912, and Garnet and Reward by 1929.

86   Average Deficiency of Rainfall

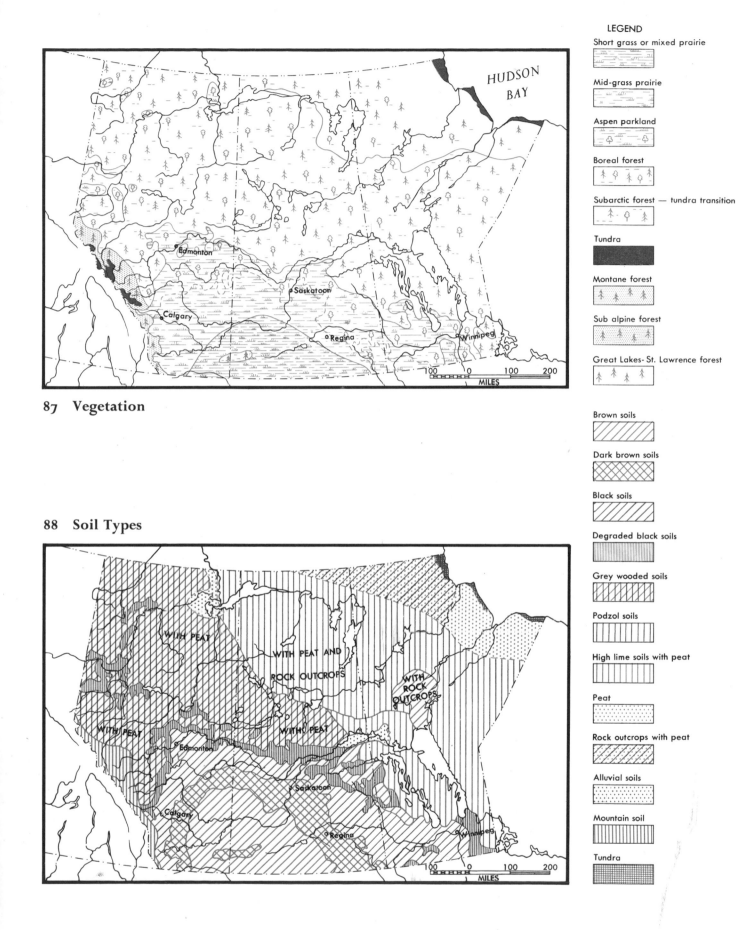

Short grass or mixed prairie

Mid-grass prairie

Aspen parkland

Boreal forest

Subarctic forest — tundra transition

Tundra

Montane forest

Sub alpine forest

Great Lakes- St. Lawrence forest

Brown soils

Dark brown soils

Black soils

Degraded black soils

Grey wooded soils

Podzol soils

High lime soils with peat

Peat

Rock outcrops with peat

Alluvial soils

Mountain soil

Tundra

87 Vegetation

88 Soil Types

HUDSON BAY

Edmonton

Saskatoon

Calgary

Regina

Winnipeg

WITH PEAT

WITH PEAT AND ROCK OUTCROPS

WITH ROCK OUTCROPS

WITH PEAT

WITH PEAT

WITH PEAT

Edmonton

Saskatoon

Calgary

Regina

Winnipeg

100 0 100 200
MILES

OPENING THE WEST AND NORTH

The Disposal of Prairie Lands

The transfer of Rupert's Land and the Northwest Territories to Canada (July 15, 1870) vested in the federal government ownership of a vast public domain five times the previous area of the whole Dominion. By terms of the transfer the Hudson's Bay Company retained blocks around the trading posts not exceeding a total of 50,000 acres and also one-twentieth of the land in a fertile belt defined as bounded by the United States, the Rocky Mountains, the North Saskatchewan, and Lake Winnipeg, Lake of the Woods and the waters linking them. The Company's twentieth eventually amounted to 6,639,059 acres. A small quantity of land

had already passed into private hands during the Hudson's Bay régime, more was set aside from time to time for Indian reservations, and generous grants were made to the half-breeds, to settlers of the Selkirk period, to members of Wolseley's expedition, and to others. There remained nevertheless enormous 'dominion lands' used by the federal government for the next sixty years for the interlocking purposes of promoting settlement and railway building. Major events in this connection occurred as follows: (1) April 25, 1871. An order in council initiated a great and almost completely uniform land survey in which each township

was six miles by six miles and contained thirty-six sections, each section containing 640 acres and being a square mile in both size and shape. Townships were numbered northward from a base line on the American border, ranges of townships east and west from a principal meridian running through Fort Garry and then, farther westward, from five other principal meridians. Sections were numbered from the south-east corner of each township. Only minor modifications were later made in this general pattern, for example, in connection with the river lots of the half-breeds on the Red, South Saskatchewan, Bow, Belly, and Red Deer Rivers and

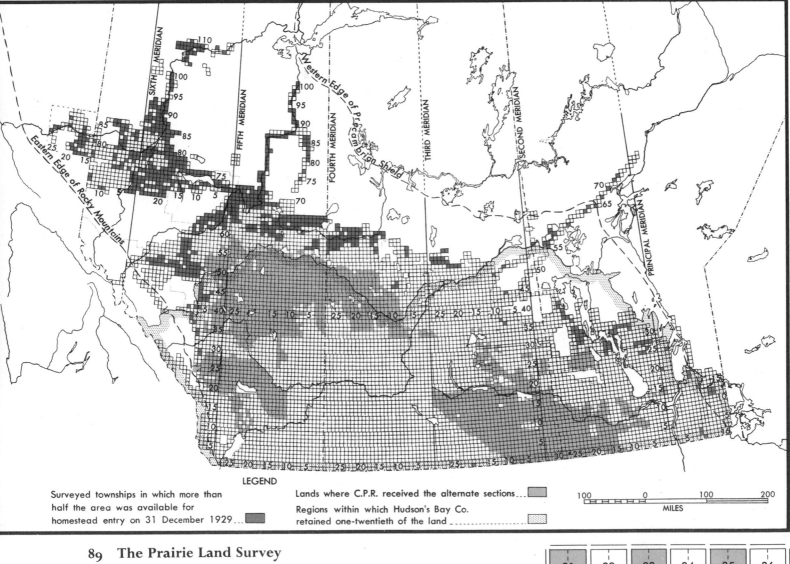

LEGEND

Surveyed townships in which more than half the area was available for homestead entry on 31 December 1929...

Lands where C.P.R. received the alternate sections...

Regions within which Hudson's Bay Co. retained one-twentieth of the land...

100   0   100   200
MILES

89   The Prairie Land Survey

90   A Prairie Township

LEGEND

Free homestead lands....

School lands............

Railway lands...........

Hudson's Bay Co. lands...

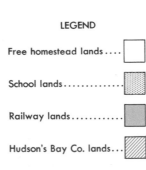

the irrigation lands of the Canadian Pacific Railway.

(2) April 14, 1872. The first Dominion Lands Act laid down basic policies including provision for free quarter-section homestead grants, reservation of sections 11 and 29 in each township to endow public schools, and allocation of section 8 and three-quarters of section 26 (the whole of 26 in every fifth township) to meet Hudson's Bay Company claims.

(3) October 21, 1880. The contract with the Canadian Pacific Railway syndicate provided, among other things, for a grant of 25,000,000 acres 'fairly fit for settlement' in the region between Winnipeg and the Rockies. In a belt 24 miles on either side of its main line the railway would have the right to alternate sections (odd-numbered sections) except for any rejected as unfit and it could make up the rest by choosing odd-numbered sections elsewhere. Modifications of these arrangements were made later, but in all, on account of main- and branch-line grants and others made to subsidiaries, the Canadian Pacific Railway eventually acquired a total of 26,055,462 acres. Grants to other 'colonization' railways totalled another 5,728,092 acres and became based on the amount that the railway could 'earn', that is, 6,400 acres in odd-numbered sections for every mile of line built.

(4) July 20, 1908. The new Dominion Lands Act included provision for liquidating the railway land-grant system. This system had served its purpose. The remaining odd-numbered sections were to be released for sale by the government. However, the revenue so obtained would be used to build the Hudson Bay Railway as a public enterprise. By 1929 when that line was completed receipts amounted to $21,992,174.

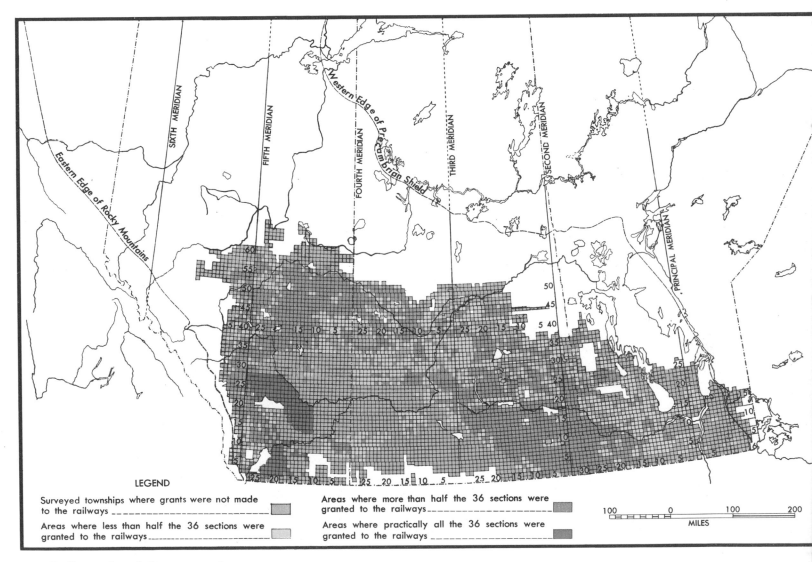

LEGEND

Surveyed townships where grants were not made to the railways _____

Areas where less than half the 36 sections were granted to the railways _____

Areas where more than half the 36 sections were granted to the railways _____

Areas where practically all the 36 sections were granted to the railways _____

100   0   100   200
MILES

91   Railway Land Grants to January 1, 1909

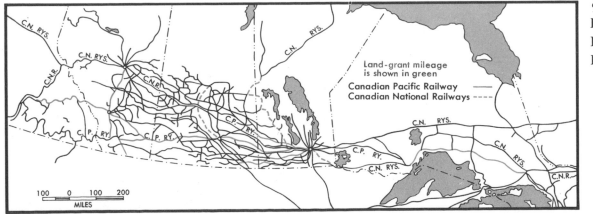

Land-grant mileage is shown in green
Canadian Pacific Railway ———
Canadian National Railways -----

100   0   100   200
MILES

92
Railways
Built under the
Land Grant System

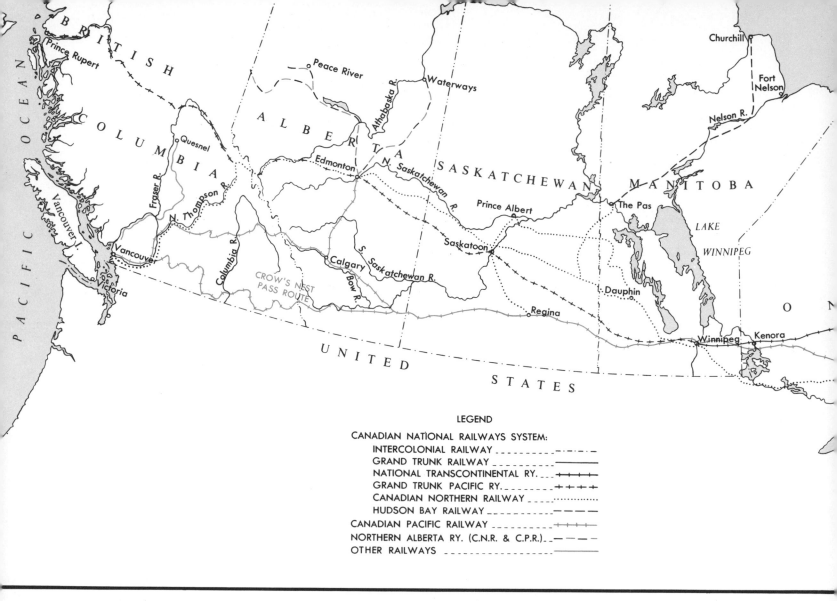

The Transportation Problem

Land grants and other aid from all levels of government were largely responsible for the rapid progress in railway building after Confederation. Total mileage in 1867 was 2,278; in 1900, 17,657; in 1914, 30,795; and in 1931, 42,280. The main line of the first transcontinental, the Canadian Pacific Railway, was completed in November, 1885. Encouraged by the flood-tide of migration to the West in the 1890's and 1900's, a railway boom took place which covered the prairies with a network of feeder lines and resulted in the emergence of two more transcontinental systems. The first, the Grand Trunk Pacific between Prince Rupert and Winnipeg, a subsidiary of the Grand Trunk, was intended to be operated in conjunction with the National Transcontinental built by the federal government from Winnipeg to

Moncton, N.B. The second, the Canadian Northern from Vancouver to Montreal, was built and pieced together by William Mackenzie and Donald Mann. Both lines were in serious difficulty by 1917 due partly to over-building and partly to the outbreak of the First World War which occurred as they were being completed and delayed further immigration and western development. Accordingly, in the period 1917–23 it became necessary for the federal government to take over the Canadian Northern, the Grand Trunk Pacific, and the Grand Trunk and consolidate them along with the government-built National Transcontinental, Intercolonial, and Prince Edward Island Railways to form the Canadian National Railways system. The Hudson Bay Railway, completed in 1929, was later added to this.

The Canadian Pacific Railway and some smaller companies remained independent.

Meanwhile, to handle the large volume of grain beginning to flow from the prairies, improvements had to be made as well in the vital St. Lawrence-Great Lakes waterway, stretching inland 2,218 miles from the Strait of Belle Isle to Port Arthur and Fort William. This involved enlarging or replacing canals built before 1850. Beginning in the 1870's, but mainly around the turn of the century, all were deepened from nine to at least fourteen feet. In addition, the ocean-shipping channel down river from Montreal was dredged to a depth of thirty (later thirty-five) feet and extensive elevator and other harbour facilities were provided at a number of ports.

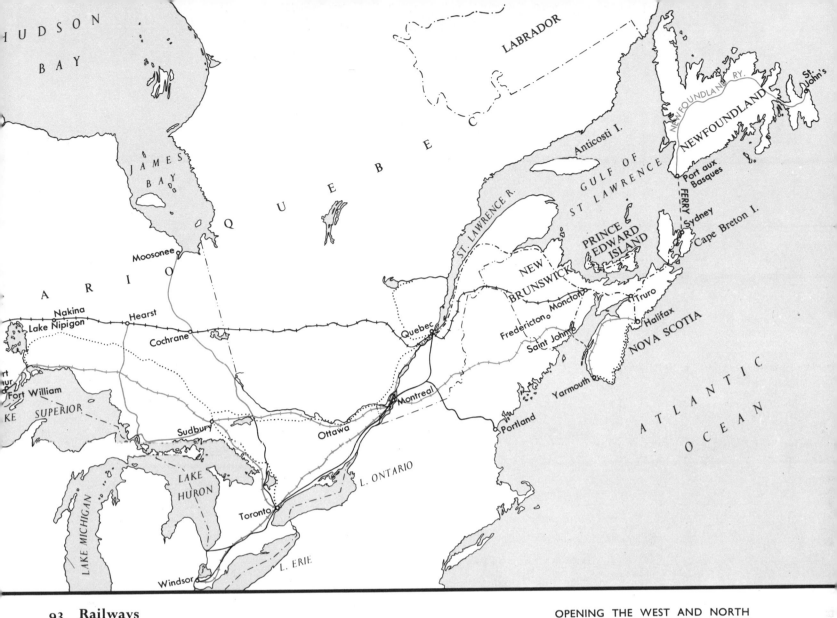

OPENING THE WEST AND NORTH

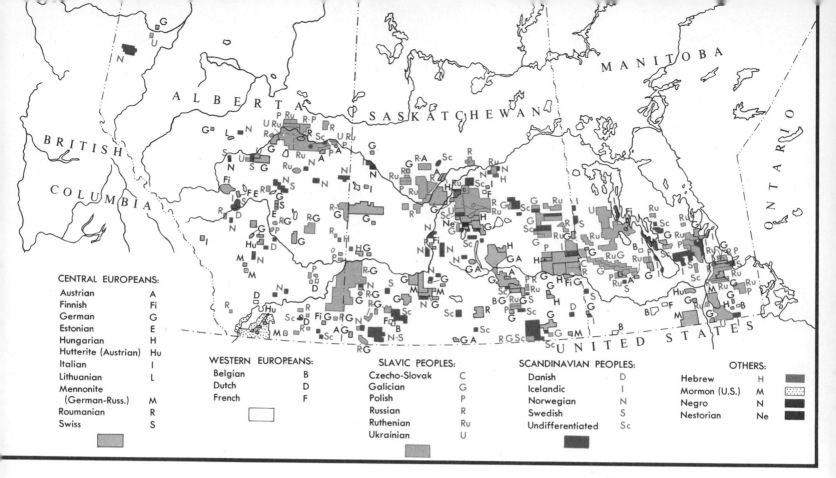

CENTRAL EUROPEANS:

Austrian	A
Finnish	Fi
German	G
Estonian	E
Hungarian	H
Hutterite (Austrian)	Hu
Italian	I
Lithuanian	L
Mennonite (German-Russ.)	M
Roumanian	R
Swiss	S

WESTERN EUROPEANS:

Belgian	B
Dutch	D
French	F

SLAVIC PEOPLES:

Czecho-Slovak	C
Galician	G
Polish	P
Russian	R
Ruthenian	Ru
Ukrainian	U

SCANDINAVIAN PEOPLES:

Danish	D
Icelandic	I
Norwegian	N
Swedish	S
Undifferentiated	Sc

OTHERS:

Hebrew	H
Mormon (U.S.)	M
Negro	N
Nestorian	Ne

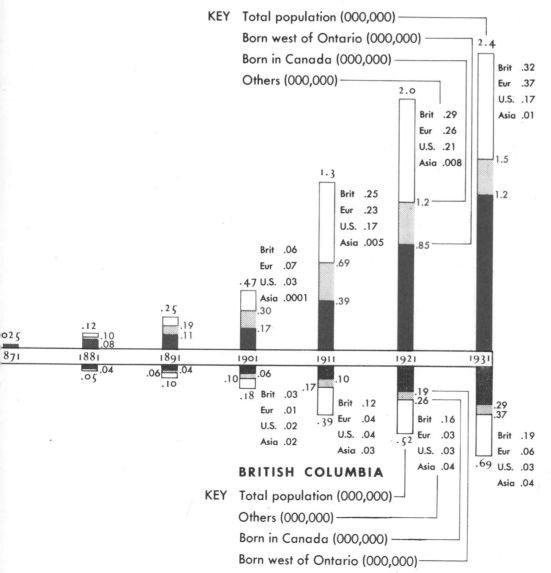

PRAIRIES

KEY
Total population (000,000)
Born west of Ontario (000,000)
Born in Canada (000,000)
Others (000,000)

1871 — .025
1881 — .12 — .10 — .08 — .04 — .05
1891 — .25 — .19 — .11 — .06 — .04 — .10
1901 — .47 — Brit .06 / Eur .07 / U.S. .03 / Asia .0001 — .30 — .17 — .18 — Brit .03 / Eur .01 / U.S. .02 / Asia .02 — .10 — .06
1911 — 1.3 — Brit .25 / Eur .23 / U.S. .17 / Asia .005 — .69 — .39 — .17 — .39 — Brit .12 / Eur .04 / U.S. .04 / Asia .03 — .10
1921 — 2.0 — Brit .29 / Eur .26 / U.S. .21 / Asia .008 — 1.2 — .85 — .52 — Brit .16 / Eur .03 / U.S. .03 / Asia .04 — .19 — .26
1931 — 2.4 — Brit .32 / Eur .37 / U.S. .17 / Asia .01 — 1.5 — 1.2 — .69 — Brit .19 / Eur .06 / U.S. .03 / Asia .04 — .29 — .37

BRITISH COLUMBIA

KEY
Total population (000,000)
Others (000,000)
Born in Canada (000,000)
Born west of Ontario (000,000)

96 The Growth and Origins of Population

Gradual completion of railways, increasing scarcity of new land in the United States, and the encouragement afforded immigration by agencies of the government and the railway companies were major factors causing an accelerated growth of population in the Canadian West in the late nineteenth and early twentieth centuries. A high proportion of the immigrants were from various European countries and many settled in separate national groups. Differing from the majority in language, traditions, and frequently in religion, these 'New Canadians' tended to be slow in assimilation and to give the prairie population a distinctive character. In British Columbia, Asiatic immigration as well was significant.

The Administration of the West and North

Following the transfer of Rupert's Land and the Northwest Territories to Canada (July 15, 1870), the province of Manitoba was created as provided for in the Manitoba Act (May 12, 1870) and the administration of the remaining unorganized Northwest

Territories was undertaken by a lieutenant-governor appointed by the federal government. Part of this region became the separate District of Keewatin in 1876. A further transfer from Britain to Canada of the Arctic Islands took place on September 1, 1880.

On July 1, 1881, the boundaries of Manitoba were enlarged somewhat and on the east they became common with the western border of Ontario. This led to a renewal of Ontario's long-standing claim to western and northern territories far beyond the limits the Canadian government was willing to acknowledge—a claim based on earlier disputes going back to French Canada and the Hudson's Bay Company and to the Quebec Act and Guy Carleton's commission as governor (see Map 42). The question had been submitted to arbitrators in 1878 but their award had not been accepted by the federal government. In 1884, it was taken before the Judicial Committee of the Privy Council which upheld the 1878 award. Eventually, in 1889, the Committee's decision was embodied in an Imperial act adding considerably to the previously recognized area of Ontario. A Canadian act of 1898 made a corresponding addition to the size of Quebec extending its boundary northward to the Eastmain River. Meanwhile, in 1882 a Canadian order in council had created the provisional districts of Assiniboia, Saskatchewan, Athabaska, and Alberta and provided for their government by a lieutenant-governor with his capital at Regina in Saskatchewan. A further order in council in 1895 created similar districts of Ungava, Franklin, Mackenzie, and Yukon, while one in 1897 made alterations in their boundaries and in those of the District of Keewatin as well. Following the discovery of gold on the Klondike (August, 1896), the District of Yukon was more fully organized as the separate Yukon Territory on June 13, 1898.

By 1905, growth of population in the prairie region was such that two new provinces, Saskatchewan and Alberta, were created. The District of Keewatin, governed to that time by the lieutenant-governor of Manitoba, was incorporated into the Northwest Territories. In 1912, the boundaries of Manitoba, Ontario, and Quebec were enlarged to their present limits.

Further changes in the boundaries of the Mackenzie, Keewatin, and Franklin Districts came into effect in 1920, the Quebec-Labrador boundary was defined by the Judicial Committee of the Privy Council in 1927, and by 1931 Canada's territorial claims extended to the North Pole.

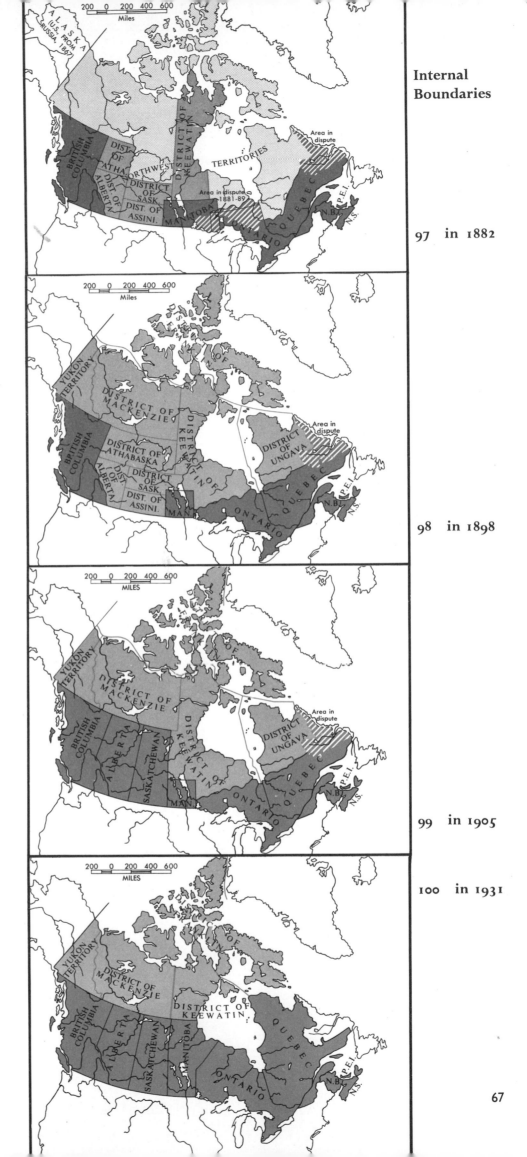

Internal Boundaries

97 in 1882

98 in 1898

99 in 1905

100 in 1931

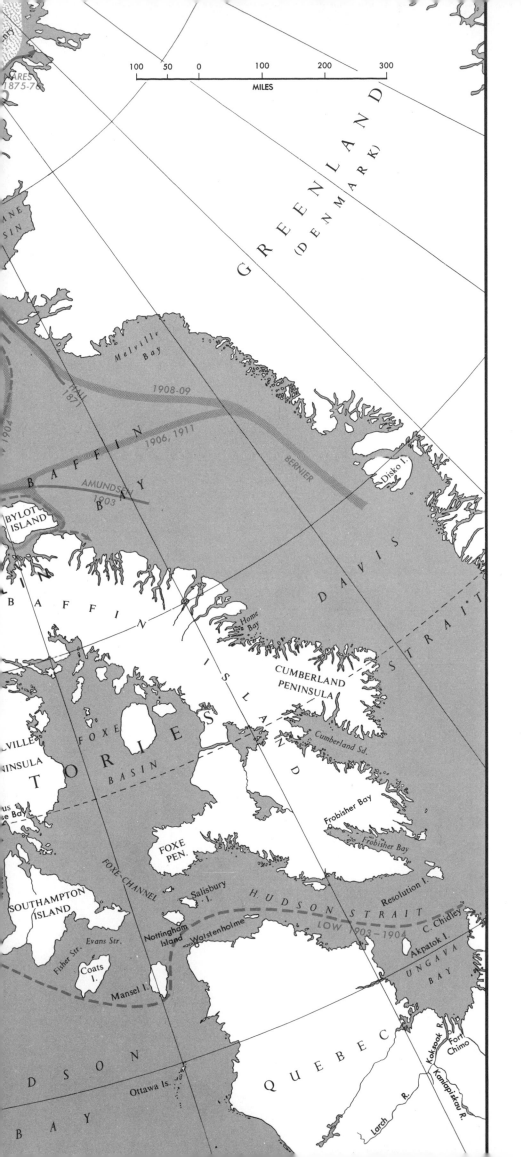

Commercial and scientific, political and personal motives led to a renewal of interest in
the Arctic beginning in the last quarter of
the nineteenth century. Whaling fleets
operating in Baffin Bay on the east and the
Beaufort Sea on the west became increasingly familiar with adjacent coasts and inlets,
while the Hudson's Bay Company, followed
shortly by a few private traders, began
opening Arctic trading posts, the first at
Wolstenholme in 1909. British, American,
Norwegian, Canadian, and other expeditions
—only a few of which can be shown on a
single map—added gradually to knowledge
of the region. Many leaders, including the
British Admiralty's Nares (1875), hoped to
be the first to reach the North Pole. This
was finally done by Peary of the American
Navy (1909). Norway's Amundsen realized
(1903–6), at the cost of three Arctic winters,
the other old dream of navigating a North-
west Passage.

From the days of Henry Hudson, however,
initial discoveries had been British (Sverdrup's Norwegian expedition, 1898–1902,
would constitute the sole major exception)
and Britain's claim to sovereignty in the
North American Arctic west of Greenland
had therefore long been recognized. After
September 1, 1880, when Britain transferred
her rights to Canada, the latter's interest became paramount. Canadian Government
expeditions under such men as Tyrrell, Low,
Bernier, and Stefansson then began collect-
ing the detailed navigational and scientific
information on which future Arctic advances
could be based.

OPENING THE WEST AND NORTH

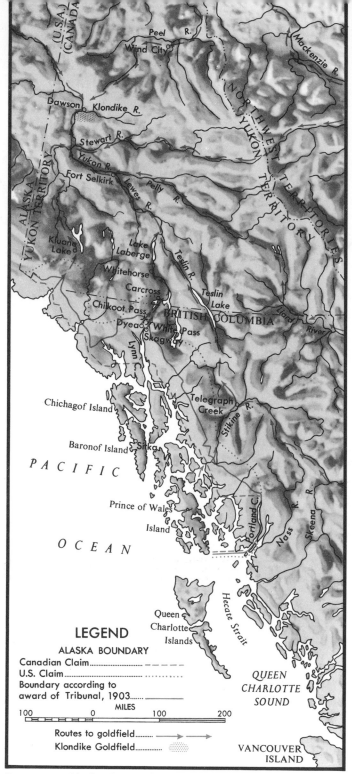

Base map copyright Canadian Aero Service Limited, Ottawa

102 Klondike Gold and the Alaska Boundary

The last great gold rush followed reports in August, 1896, of discoveries in Bonanza Creek, a tributary of the Klondike near Dawson City. In the next few years miners poured in, mainly by ship up the Lynn Canal to Dyea or Skagway and thence through the Chilkoot and White Passes and down 500 miles of the Lewes and Yukon Rivers to Dawson. Others made their way up the Stikine River or even by way of the Mackenzie and Porcupine. Dawson rapidly acquired a population of 25,000 and annual gold production rose to a maximum, in 1900, of over a million and a quarter fine ounces.

Rival claims of Canada and the United States to the ports at the head of the Lynn Canal, based on differing interpretations of the Anglo-Russian Treaty of 1825 (see Map 57), became of immediate importance. They were finally settled in favour of the United States by a joint Anglo-American tribunal appointed in 1903 to define the whole Canada-Alaska boundary. Two of the three British arbitrators were Canadians who dissented from the majority decision.

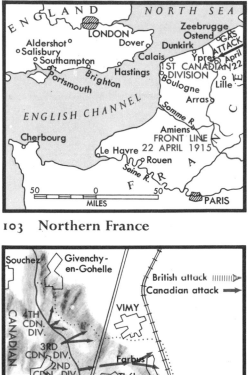

103   Northern France

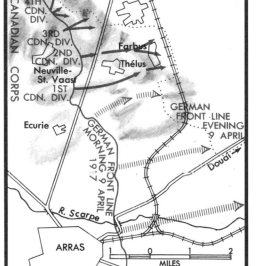

104   Vimy, 1917

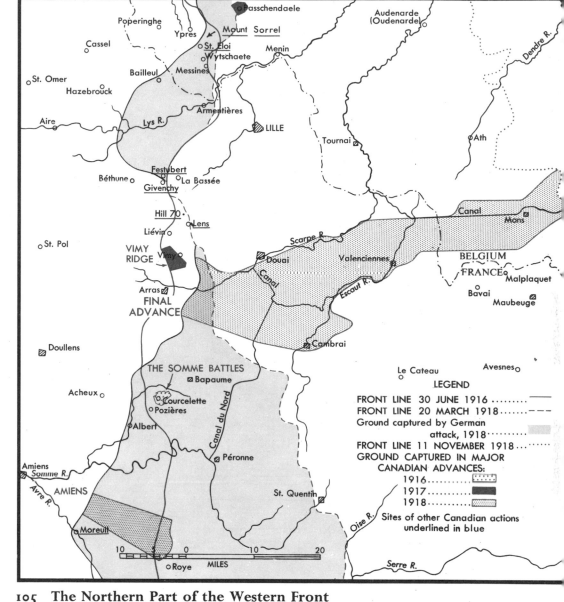

105   The Northern Part of the Western Front

The First World War

Canada entered the First World War automatically when Britain did on August 4, 1914, and the First Canadian Contingent, 33,000 strong, embarked for overseas service two months later (October 3). Others followed and a Canadian Corps was eventually formed under the successive commands of Lieutenant-General E. A. H. Alderson, Lieutenant-General Sir Julian Byng, and finally of the first Canadian, Lieutenant-General Sir Arthur Currie (June 23, 1917).

1915. The Canadians' battle experience began with the famous defensive struggle commonly called the Second Battle of Ypres (April 22–7) when they held their line in spite of the Germans' first use of poison gas. Fighting at Festubert and Givenchy (May 20–6) followed with heavy losses.

1916. The Canadians took part in engagements at St. Eloi (April 3–20) and Mount Sorrel (June 1–3) before being transferred in August from Flanders to the Somme to assist in the great and futile allied offensive there, their only real success being the cap-ture of Courcelette (September 15).

1917. The taking of Vimy Ridge (April 9), the first occasion when all four Canadian divisions attacked together, was followed by victory at Hill 70 (August 15) and the bloody battle for Passchendaele (October 26–November 10).

1918. After a major success at Amiens (August 8) the Canadians broke through the Drocourt-Quéant line (September 2–4), took Cambrai (October 1–9), and were in Mons when the Armistice came (November 11).

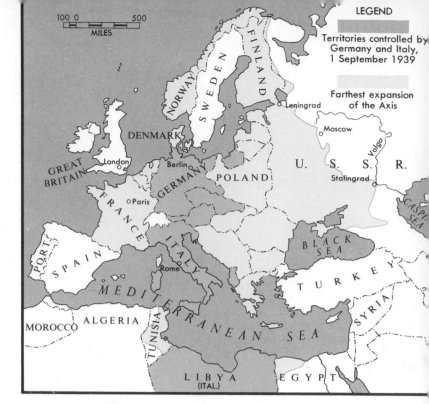

106 **Axis Domination of Europe, 1942**

107 **The Battle of the Atlantic**

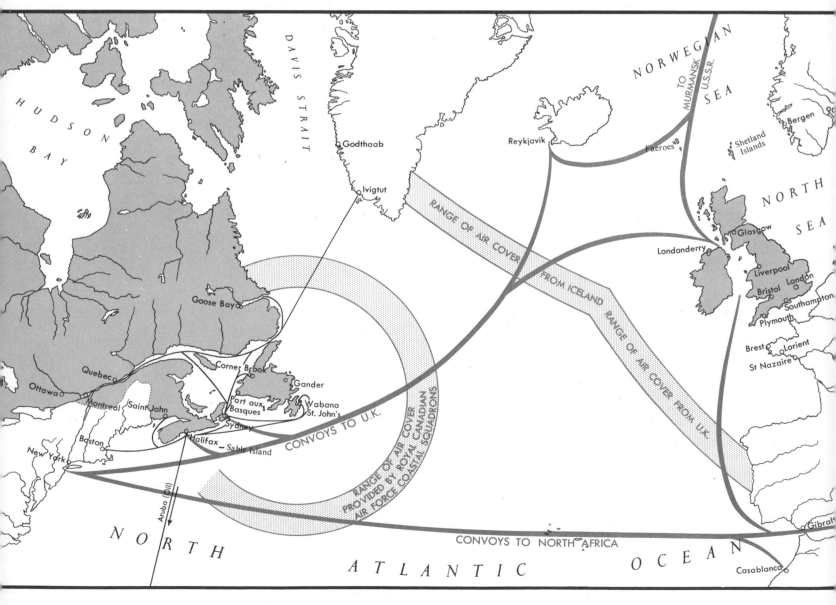

The Second World War

Germany's invasion of Poland on September 1, 1939, led to declarations of war by Britain and France (September 3) and various other allied powers including Canada (September 10). Already in occupation of Austria and Czechoslovakia, the Germans swept rapidly through Poland, entered Denmark and Norway (April 9, 1940), defeated the Low Countries and France, which signed an Armistice (June 22, 1940), and invaded Russia (June 21, 1941). Meanwhile they had been joined by the Italians (June 10, 1940) and when on December 7, 1941, the Japanese struck at the American base of Pearl Harbour and British and Dutch possessions in the Far East the conflict became world-wide. By mid-1942, almost the whole of Europe and North Africa was under the domination of the Rome-Berlin Axis while much of the Pacific, south-east Asia, and China were controlled by Japan.

A major contribution of the Canadian navy throughout the war was helping to protect, with her corvettes, frigates, and other escort vessels, the life-stream of supplies and reinforcements flowing from North America to Britain across the cold, stormy, and U-boat-infested North Atlantic. The air force shared in this task, in the great Commonwealth Air Training Plan based in Canada, and in allied fighting, bombing, and reconnaissance generally.

The army's first major opportunity came with the invasion of Sicily. Canadian forces joined the British and Americans, fresh from victories in North Africa, to help capture that island (July–August, 1943) and cross to the mainland of Italy (September 3). In heavy street fighting during the Christmas season they drove the Germans out of Ortona (December 21–8). The next spring, the First Canadian Corps broke the Adolf Hitler Line across the Liri valley (May 23). In the autumn, back on the Adriatic Coast, it breached the Gothic Line along the Foglia River (August 30–September 3) and entered the broad Po Valley where the line was stabilized for the winter. The First Corps moved to north-west Europe early in 1945.

108 **The Italian Campaign**

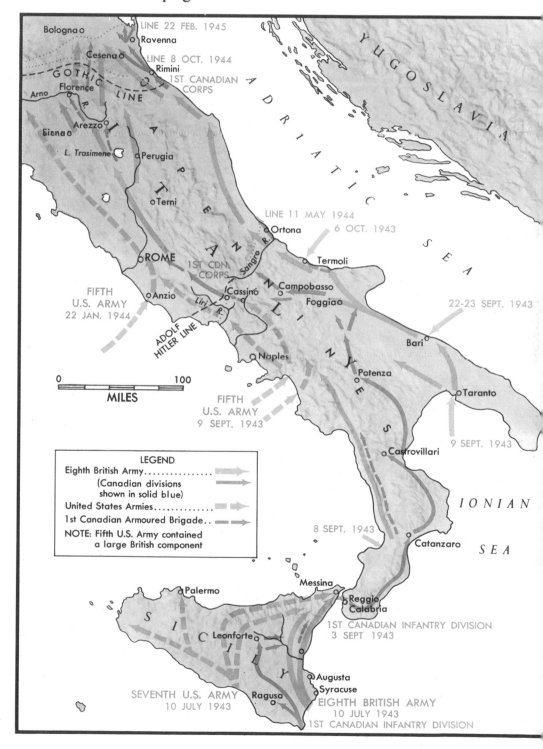

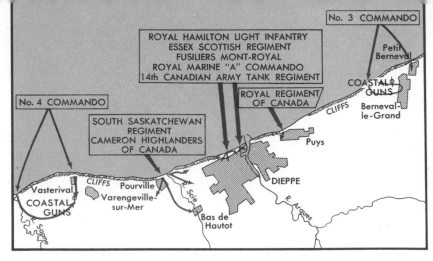

109 The Dieppe Raid

110 Invasion and Victory

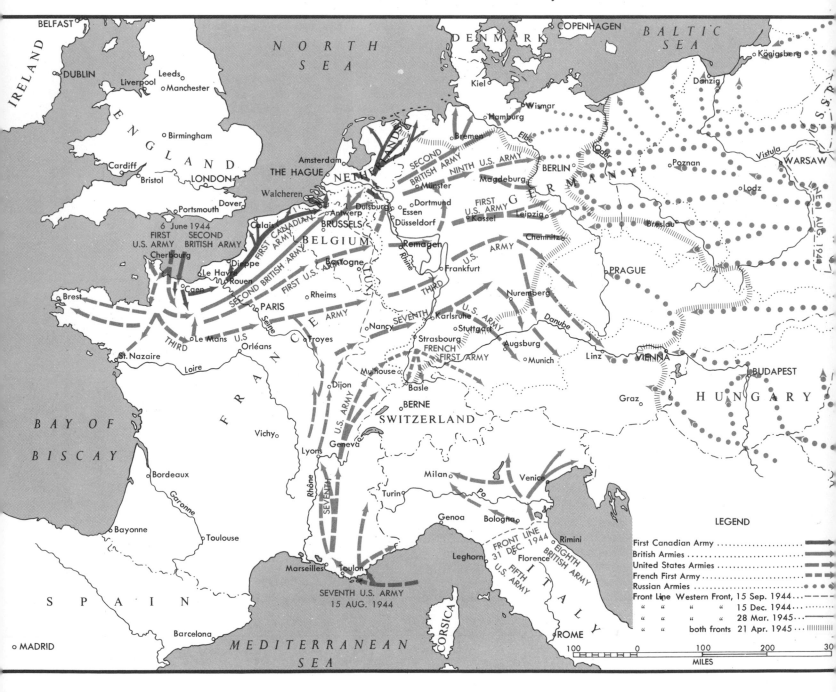

A landing craft

The Dieppe Raid (August 19, 1942), undertaken by Canadians, supported by British commando units to which some American and Free French soldiers were attached, tried the strength of Hitler's continental defences. It cost Canada 3,350 casualties out of some 5,000 participants.

This lesson was not forgotten in the elaborate planning that preceded the final allied landings in Normandy (June 6, 1944). One Canadian division took part in these and in the strategically important capture of Caen (July 9). Soon afterwards the First Canadian Army became operational (July 23) and by hard persistent fighting took Falaise (August 17) helping, along with the Americans at Argentan, to close the gap through which the Germans had hoped to escape from their lost battlefields of Normandy.

Turning north-eastward along the allied left flank, the Canadians went on to clear the Channel ports (including Dieppe), eliminate flying-bomb sites, and finally wear down German resistance in South Beveland and Walcheren, opening the Scheldt and its vital port of Antwerp by November 28.

Remaining on the flank when the last great allied offensive began in February, 1945, they battered stubbornly through the defences of the Reichswald and Hochwald region until, with the allied crossing of the Rhine in several sectors, German strength began to crumble. Mopping-up operations in the northern Netherlands and adjacent parts of Germany concluded with the German surrender on May 7.

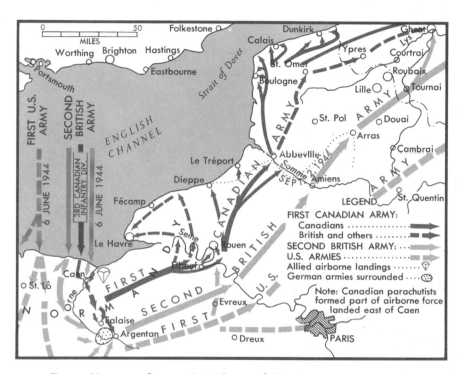

111   From Normandy to the Channel Ports

112   The Netherlands and German Campaigns

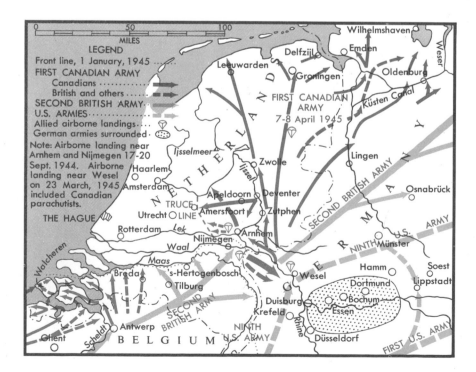

ARMED FORCES (000 men)

KEY
- Canadian Expeditionary Force
- Navy
- Fatal casualties (army)
  Total fatal casualties: Army: 59,544;
  Navy: 142; with R.F.C., R.N.A.S.
  & R.A.F.: 1,563, some of whom are
  included in the figure for the army.

KEY
Fatal casualties (army); total for war: 22,817
- Army
- Navy (total fatal casualties: 2,019)
- R.C.A.F.
- Fatal casualties (R.C.A.F.); total for war: 17,1

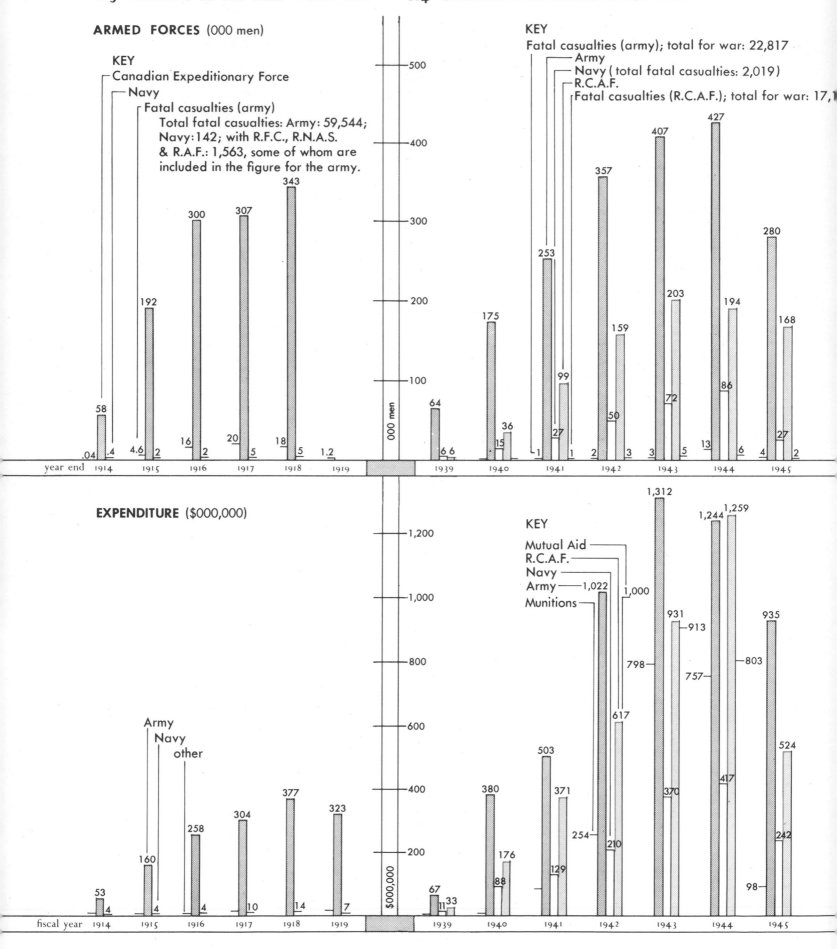

EXPENDITURE ($000,000)

Army
Navy
other

KEY
Mutual Aid
R.C.A.F.
Navy
Army
Munitions

Newfoundland's union with Canada was proposed at the time of the original Confederation discussions in the 1860's, again after a disastrous bank failure in 1894, and once more during the First World War. All change was resisted however until 1934 when, as a result of financial collapse brought on by the depression, the eighty-year-old system of Responsible Government had to be abandoned and Newfoundland reverted to colonial status under a Commission of Government appointed by Britain. During the Second World War the establishment of Canadian and American air and naval bases brought unprecedented prosperity. Afterwards the question arose: Should Newfoundland's independence be restored or should she join Canada or possibly the United States? The answer was given when on March 31, 1949, Newfoundland became Canada's tenth province.

The island's economy, dependent from the earliest days on the fisheries, had always lacked stability. The remedy of diversification was difficult to achieve. Soil and climate forbade all but the most modest amount of agriculture. Iron mining, which began on Bell Island in 1895, and the building of the Corner Brook paper mill in 1925 were the two most hopeful signs of progress. The meandering trans-island railway, completed from St. John's to Port aux Basques in 1897, helped open the interior but remained a constant financial burden. In 1923, it had to be taken over by the government, along with essential steamship and telegraph services. Second World War prosperity, however, and Confederation seemed likely to produce an upward trend, especially since the Confederation Agreement included provision for quite large federal subsidies, federal maintenance of certain transportation facilities, and federal acceptance of responsibility for the existing provincial debt. At the same time technological and other changes were creating new opportunities (and some new problems) for the fishing industry and in connection with the fuller utilization of the mineral and forest resources of the interior and also of Labrador.

115 Confederation with Newfoundland

ARCTIC

OCEAN

U.S. submarine "Nautilus" from Point Barrow, 1 August 1958 under ice
to North Pole (3 August) and on to Atlantic Ocean between Spitsbergen
and Greenland (5 August).

QUEEN   ELIZABETH

ISLANDS

BEAUFORT

SEA

Meighen I.

AXEL
HEIBERG
ISLAND

Eureka

Borden I.

Prince Gustaf Adolf Sea

SVERDRUP   ISLANDS

Ellef
Ringnes
I.

Amund
Ringnes
I.

ELLESMERE   ISLAND

Norwegian
Bay

Grise Fiord

Alexandra
Fiord

Nansen Sound

Mackenzie
King I.

Cornwall I.

PRINCE
PATRICK I.

Maud
Bay

HAZEN STRAIT

PARRY   ISLANDS

Belcher Chan.

Jones Sound

DEVON ISLAND

APPROXIMATE LIMIT OF PERMANENT POLAR ICE

McClure Str.

MELVILLE   ISLAND

"ST-ROCH"

BATHURST I.

VISCOUNT

PARRY   CHANNEL

LANCASTER SOU

Cornwallis I.   Resolute

Wellington Chan.

BANKS
ISLAND

Sachs Harbour

Prince of Wales Str.

MELVILLE SOUND

Stefansson
I.

Peel Sd.

SOMERSET
ISLAND

BRODEUR PEN.

Prince Regent In.

USA.
CANADA

Mackenzie

Bay Tuktoyaktuk

WINTER
1940-41

"ST-ROCH" 1940-42
AMUNDSEN
Cape
Parry

GULF

1944

DISTRICT

PRINCE
OF
WALES
ISLAND

M'CLINTOCK CHAN.

OF
FRAN

Bellot Str.

Old Crow

Aklavik

Reindeer Depot

Fort
McPherson

Arctic Red
River

Inuvik

Anderson R.

Prince Albert Sd.

VICTORIA

WOLLASTON

Holman I. PEN.

ISLAND

GULF

OF

BOOTHIA

Peel R.

Fort Good Hope

Mackenzie

Dolphin and Union

Read I.

Victoria Str.

James Ross Str.

WINTER
1941-42

BOOTHIA
PEN.

Spence

Norman Wells

Horton R.

Coppermine

Coronation Gulf

Cambridge
Bay

KING
WILLIAM
I. Gjoa
Haven

Pelly Ba

Pelly Bay

Fort Franklin
Great Bear
R.

Great Bear
Lake

Port Radium

Coppermine R.

Hood R.

Queen Maud Gulf

"ST-ROCH"

Chantrey In.

Fort Norman

Sawmill Bay

Perry River

Camsell R.

Bathurst Inlet

ARCTIC CIRCLE

YUKON   TERRITORY

DISTRICT   OF   MACKENZIE

NORTHWEST   TERRI

Contwoyto L.

Pelly L.

Schultz L.

Baker
Lake

Chesterfield Inlet

DISTRICT   OF   KEEWATIN

Wrigley

Point L.

Back R.

Garry L. Macdougall

Baker L.

Chesterville Inlet

South
Nahanni R.

Lac La
Martre

RIVER

Aylmer L.
Clinton
Colden
Lake

Thelon R.

Wharton L.

Dubawnt L.

Watson
Lake

Nahanni Butte

Fort
Simpson

Rae

Discovery

Artillery L.

Dubawnt R.

Rankin Inlet

BRITISH   COLUMBIA

Beatton River

Liard River

Fort Liard

Jean-
Marie R.

Fort
Providence

Yellowknife

Fort Reliance

Snowdrift

Kazan R.

Whale Cove

ALASKA
HIGHWAY

Hay River

Great Slave
Lake

Rocher
River

Taltson R.

Maguse River

Eskimo Point

Hard Rock

MACKENZIE HWY.

Hay
River

Fort Resolution

Fort Smith

Wholdaia L.

Kasba L.

Tha-anne R.

Fort Nelson

Great Slave

Selwyn L.

Nueltin Lake

LBERTA

Uranium City

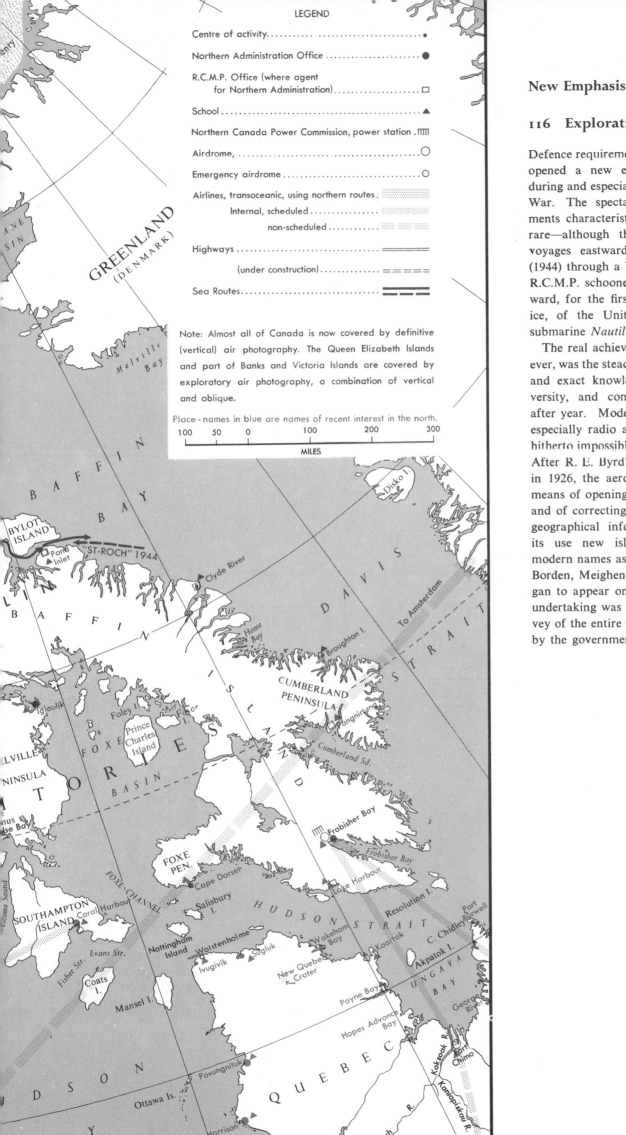

New Emphasis on the North

116 Exploration and Mapping

Defence requirements and scientific advances opened a new era of Arctic exploration during and especially after the Second World War. The spectacular individual achievements characteristic of earlier periods were rare—although they included the famous voyages eastward (1940–2) and westward (1944) through a North-west Passage by the R.C.M.P. schooner *St. Roch,* and that eastward, for the first time beneath the Arctic ice, of the United States Navy's atomic submarine *Nautilus* (1958).

The real achievement of this period, however, was the steady accumulation of detailed and exact knowledge by government, university, and commercial expeditions year after year. Modern devices and equipment, especially radio and the aeroplane, allowed hitherto impossible feats to be accomplished. After R. E. Byrd's flight over the Pole itself in 1926, the aeroplane rapidly became the means of opening new posts and settlements and of correcting and supplementing earlier geographical information. Partly through its use new islands, identified by such modern names as Air Force, Prince Charles, Borden, Meighen, and Mackenzie King, began to appear on maps. The largest single undertaking was an airborne geological survey of the entire Canadian Arctic completed by the government in the 1950's.

RECENT DEVELOPMENTS

ARCTIC OCEAN

BEAUFORT SEA

QUEEN ELIZABETH ISLANDS

ALASKA (U.S.A.)

Fairbanks

Yukon R.

YUKON OIL

TUNGSTEN
Fort McPherson
Aklavik
Inuvik
Arctic Red River

ASBESTOS
LEAD
ZINC
GOLD
Dawson
Keno Hill
GOLD SILVER LEAD
ZINC CADMIUM
Mayo Landing
Ross River

NICKEL
COPPER
Kluane
GOLD
COAL
LEAD
TERRITORY
COAL
MOLYBDENUM
TUNGSTEN
ZINC GOLD

Whitehorse
Teslin
TIN
TIN
Haines
Skagway
White Pass
Porter ASBESTOS
Alaska Highway

Telegraph Creek

Wrangell

Prince Rupert
Sandspit

BRITISH
SILVER
LEAD
ZINC
CADMIUM
Kitimat
(Aluminum)

COLUMBIA

Bridge River
GOLD

Prince
George
Barkerville
Gold

Vancouver
Victoria

VANCOUVER ISLAND
TO ORIENT

PACIFIC OCEAN

Fort Good Hope

Norman Wells
OIL

DISTRICT
OF
MACKENZIE
OIL

Fort Simpson
GOLD

Fort Providence

Fort St. John
GAS
Grimshaw
Peace River
N.A. Rys.
OIL
GAS

ALBERTA
OIL

Edmonton
Nickel
Copper
GAS

Calgary

Tête Jaune
C.N.R.
C.P.R.
P.G.E. Ry.

Parry Point

Coppermine
COPPER

Port Radium
URANIUM
RADIUM
SILVER
Great Bear Lake

Snare River
URANIUM
Rae
Yellowknife
GOLD

Great Slave Lake
Fort Resolution
ZINC LEAD NICKEL
Hay River

Fort Reliance
COPPER

Road portage for river traffic

Fort Smith
Fort Fitzgerald

Peace R.
Fort Vermilion

McMurray
Waterways

Athabaska R.

Uranium City
Stony Rapids
Lake Athabaska

Wollaston
Brochet

Cree
Lake

La Ronge

Prince Albert

SASKATCHEWAN

Saskatoon

Regina

GOLD
DISTRICT

Cambridge Bay
COPPER

GOLD
COPPER
NICKEL

GOLD
GOLD

Baker Lake

DISTRICT
OF
KEEWATIN

Chesterfield Inlet
NICKEL COPPER
Rankin Inlet

Tavani
COPPER
NICKEL
IRON
Eskimo Point

GOLD
COPPER

Churchill

TO VANCOUVER

Lynn
Lake
NICKEL COPPER
COBALT

Flin
Flon
(Copper, Zinc
Cadmium)

ZINC
COPPER
Cadmium

The Pas

Hudson Bay

Dauphin

GOLD

Mystery
Lake
NICKEL

Norway
House

MANITOBA

Lake
Winnipeg

Winnipeg

Resolute

FRANKLIN

Grise
Fiord

Spence
Bay

Gjoa
Haven

LEAD
ZINC
Arctic Bay

Pond
Inlet

BAFFIN

IRON
Cape
Dorset

Coral
Harbour

HUDSON
BAY

Port Harrison

York Factory

Fort Severn

Winisk

IRON
BELCHER IS.

Fort George

ONTARIO

GOLD
Pickle Crow

GOLD
Red Lake

Sioux Lookout
C.P.R.
C.N.R.

Steep
Rock
Lake
Port Arthur

Fort Albany

Moosonee

Fort George

Nakina
Cochrane
Porcupine
C.P.R.
Sudbury

LEGEND

COMMUNICATIONS

Railways (major transcontinental
and northern)..............................

(under construction)..............

Highways (northern)..............................

(under construction)..............

Winter tractor Roads..............................

Airlines, transoceanic, using northern routes..

Internal, scheduled..............................

non-scheduled..............

Water transportation routes.................

Inland water transportation routes.............

Route of Eastern Arctic Patrol (annual)........

RESOURCES AND DEVELOPMENT

Oil or gas field..............................

Mine..............................

Pipelines..............................

Smelters or refineries...................(Aluminum)

Power stations (Northern Canada Power Commission)....

SCALE   100   0   100   200   300

MILES

80

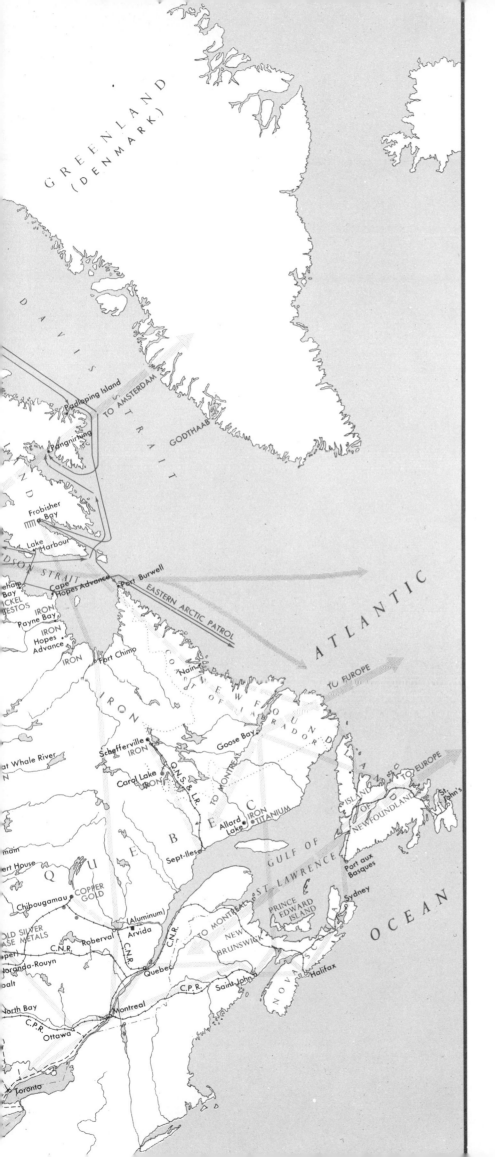

First explored largely in the interests of the fur trade, the northern parts of Canada long had little other economic value. In a few areas, notably the Peace River country settled in the 1920's and 1930's, agriculture proved surprisingly successful, but its general significance was bound to remain limited.

As early as the eighteenth century minerals were known to exist, as for example at the mouth of Samuel Hearne's Coppermine River, and attempts had been made from time to time to work some of them. Their large-scale exploitation, however, had to await improvements in transportation and communication, notably the coming of the railway, aeroplane, and radio.

The first northward step was taken when the transcontinental railway building of the late nineteenth and early twentieth centuries incidentally opened up important mineral regions in the Canadian Shield and the Rockies, mainly in Quebec, Ontario, British Columbia, and Manitoba. The great metal belt from Sudbury to Cobalt and Porcupine was an especially valuable part of this ' Old North ' of the 1920's.

The commercial opening of the Norman Wells oil field in 1920 and the discovery of pitchblende at Port Radium on Great Bear Lake in 1930 foreshadowed the period after the Second World War when the farther north, opened by the aeroplane, became of rapidly increasing interest. Then from the gas fields of the Peace River to the iron ore of Ungava and as far north as the remote Queen Elizabeth Islands, claims were staked and in many places major development began. With the establishment of towns and trade, waterways, new roads, and railways were needed to supplement the aeroplane.

RECENT DEVELOPMENTS

118 Continental Defence and NATO

In addition to mineral discoveries, continental defence requirements were responsible for much of the attention paid to northern Canada after the Second World War. In this period world power was centred round two great nuclei, the United States and Russia, and attack by the latter across the North Pole rapidly became feasible through the development of long-range bombers and later intercontinental ballistic missiles. Being in the direct line of any such attack, Canada's defence role took on an entirely new character. The North Atlantic Treaty Organization, which Canada had helped form in 1949 along with the United States, Britain, and a number of western European countries, mainly with a view to the defence of the latter, now had to be supplemented by increasing emphasis on defence of the North American continent itself. Among the steps taken for this purpose was the construction in Canada of three lines of radar stations to give advance warning of an enemy air attack. The first, the Pinetree Line, became fully operational in 1954 and consisted of thirty-four stations, twenty-two built by the United States. It was followed by the McGill Fence or Mid-Canada Line undertaken by Canada, and finally by the American-financed Distant Early Warning Line, in use by 1957.

RECENT DEVELOPMENTS

LEGEND

Independent countries of Commonwealth
Principal insular territories, dependencies, colonies and protectorates
Mandates, trust territories shown thus or with name underlined thus

GHANA
GILBERT IS.
TANGANYIKA TERR.
WESTERN SAMOA

84

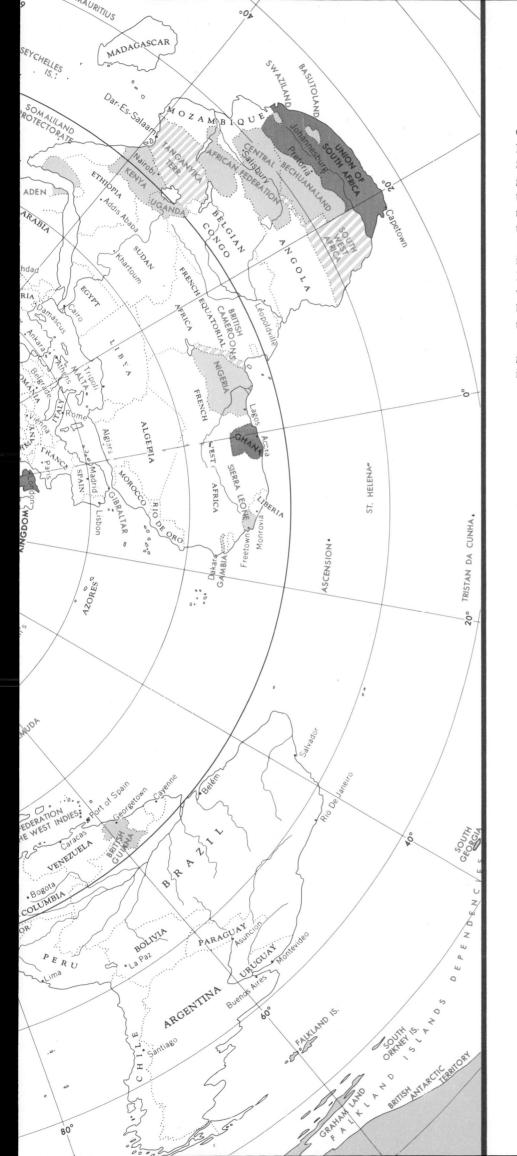

119 The Commonwealth
(January 1, 1960)

Canada's new military commitments in NATO and directly with the United States were not the only features of her growing participation in world affairs as the twentieth century went on. An independent nation within the Commonwealth following the passage of the Statute of Westminster in 1931, she continued to have special, though increasingly intangible, ties not only with Britain and the older Dominions, but also with the emerging Asian and African members, such as India, Pakistan, and Ghana. In the larger United Nations founded June 26, 1945, Canada was a member from the beginning and at times took an important part in its discussions.

RECENT DEVELOPMENTS

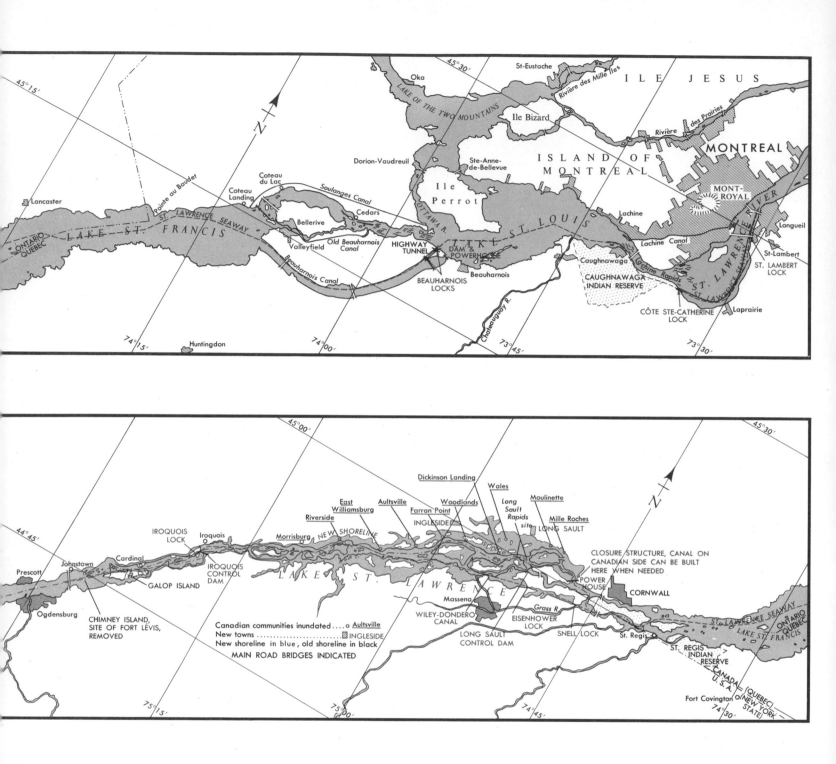

120 The St. Lawrence Seaway

The official opening of the St. Lawrence Seaway on June 26, 1959, by Queen Elizabeth II and President Eisenhower, celebrated the completion of a very large construction project which enabled ocean shipping to penetrate over two thousand miles from the Atlantic to the heart of the continent. The major task had been to replace outmoded fourteen-foot canals and locks in the St. Lawrence between Montreal and Lake Ontario by new ones twenty-seven feet in depth. Seven new locks were built to replace twenty-one smaller ones, five by Canada and two by the United States. Seven bridges between Montreal and Lake St. Francis were modified to give ship clearance of 120 feet, and the building of others was undertaken.

Associated with the navigation project was a huge new power development undertaken at the same time in the international rapids section between Cornwall and Prescott. It provided over two million horse-power of electrical energy to be divided equally between Canada and the United States.

PART SIX

MAIN ECONOMIC AND POLITICAL TRENDS SINCE 1867

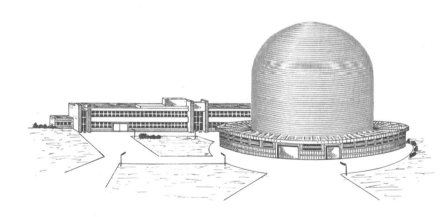

The Canada-India NRX-type atomic reactor

SECTION I   THE GROWTH OF THE ECONOMY

Introduction

The diagrams on the facing and following pages summarize main features of Canada's economic development since Confederation. At first glance they may look forbiddingly complex, but in fact most conform to a similar and quite easily understandable pattern. For example, most have columns for the census years—every tenth year since 1871—and also 1956. Frequently the census dates are on a centre line with the columns above and below representing the same total amounts—here total populations—but the upper and lower columns are differently divided to display different sorts of information. The small bars on the right of some columns give still further information, sometimes, as in the upper columns here, information about provincial distribution. The provinces are always dealt with in the same order from the western at the top to the eastern at the bottom. Each diagram has its own explanatory 'key'.

Once the standard pattern has become familiar, the considerable amount of information that each diagram contains can be perceived without too much difficulty. The same information could have been shown on a number of separate and very simple diagrams instead of on one rather complex one, and that is the usual practice. However, while there are virtues in simplicity, there is the disadvantage in this case that without experience in the use of statistical graphs one may not be able to draw together the facts contained in a group of small separate diagrams and appreciate their significant relationships. These relationships are immediately visible in each of the present diagrams.

Whether the diagrams are simple or complex one inescapable problem remains in any statistical survey of this sort. The statistics are never absolutely accurate or complete and those of earlier or later periods are never exactly comparable with one another. This will become particularly evident in later diagrams where current and constant dollars have had to be used to compensate for the changing value of money. Even the population diagram on these pages, however, is not without its pitfalls. To mention only one: urban population was defined until the 1951 census as the population of incorporated cities, towns, and villages, but there were considerable discrepancies because each province had its own individual policy, which it might well change from time to time, regarding such incorporations. The 1951 census adopted a uniform definition for the whole country based mainly on population density. This was used in 1956 also, but not without a few further minor alterations.

Nevertheless, despite any apparent complexity and regardless of the need to allow for detailed weaknesses in the statistics themselves, the present diagrams reveal much that is highly significant about Canada's economic evolution since Confederation. And, the more carefully each is studied along with its accompanying text, the more intriguing will be found its revelations.

Population

Four basic facts about the growth in Canadian population between 1871 and 1956 are shown in the upper set of columns on this diagram: (1) the rate of that growth, which it will be noted was greatly accelerated after 1891 when the opening of the West was taking place; (2) the relative importance of natural increase and net immigration in accounting for growth, the latter factor becoming more important in recent decades—indeed there was net emigration from Canada before 1901; (3) the changing distribution of population provincially with Ontario and Quebec occupying increasing portions of successive columns until the balance began to be somewhat readjusted as a result of the rapid growth of the West; (4) the rural-urban distribution. The dotted line showing the last shows the steadily declining proportion of rural to urban population, more rapid in recent decades. It does not, even so, make clear the whole picture regarding the actual as well as relative decrease in farm population after 1931, because that decrease began to be offset somewhat by an increase in rural non-farm population, exemplified in particular by the automobile commuter with his home and family in the country and his job in an adjacent town or city.

The lower columns, except for the last, show countries of birth and national origins. The first, which is of course directly related to the immigration figures of the upper columns, indicates roughly the extent of 'Canadianization' at different periods, and the nature of the non-Canadian-born part of the population. The second is significant in a country like Canada where among British and French and to some extent other ethnic groups original national differences have tended to persist in modified form for generations after migration. The 1956 column draws attention to the factor of age distribution, important as showing among other things the proportion of people in the productive working age compared with children and old people. This proportion has changed considerably since Confederation. Then, the percentage of children was so much greater that despite the smaller percentage of old people the percentage in the working age was also smaller than in recent decades. Increased percentages of both children and old people after the Second World War began to lower the worker percentage once again. One example may be given in this connection to emphasize again the need for caution in using statistics: the farm child typical of earlier decades became economically useful much younger than does the town child of the mid-twentieth century. Age alone therefore, as shown on this diagram, cannot present the whole story.

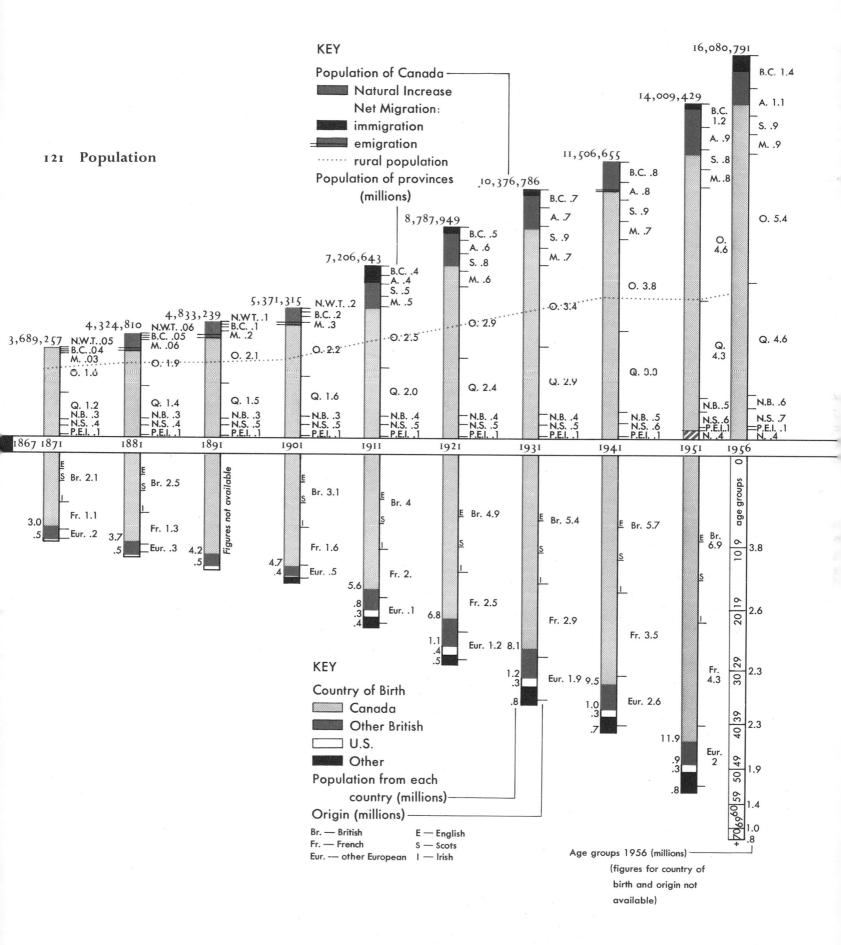

KEY

Population of Canada
- Natural Increase

Net Migration:
- immigration
- emigration
- rural population

Population of provinces (millions)

KEY

Country of Birth
- Canada
- Other British
- U.S.
- Other

Population from each country (millions)

Origin (millions)

Br. — British   E — English
Fr. — French   S — Scots
Eur. — other European   I — Irish

Age groups 1956 (millions)
(figures for country of birth and origin not available)

THE GROWTH OF THE ECONOMY

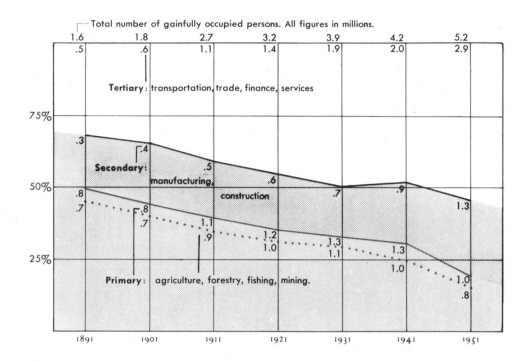

122   The Distribution of Labour

The growth in the numbers of those gainfully employed is shown in the figures along the top of the adjacent diagram which makes clear as well significant changes over the years in the distribution of labour. Not always realized is the fact that the great decline in the percentage of those engaged in agriculture and the other primary industries has been balanced not so much by an increase in employment in manufacturing and construction, although their proportion has gone up slightly, but by the remarkable rise in importance of the tertiary industries —government and other services, transportation, trade, and finance.

What the diagram does not portray are the equally significant changes that have taken place in the quality of Canada's labour force and its per capita output since Confederation. Output has gone up greatly with the use of machinery and new scientific methods and also because of such factors as higher standards of health, education, and training. The increase has not been uniform in all sectors of labour. It has, for example, been even greater in agriculture than in manufacturing because in the latter the effect of improved methods and machinery has been offset to a greater extent by reduced working hours.

All figures in billion dollars

See diagram 124
for interpretation

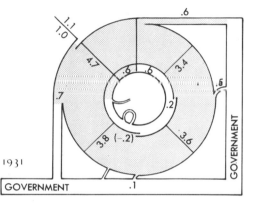

1931

GOVERNMENT

GOVERNMENT

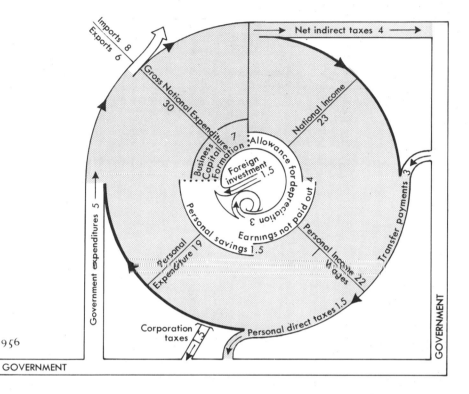

1956

GOVERNMENT

GOVERNMENT

123   The Circulation of Money in 1931   124   The Circulation of Money in 1956

The growth of the Canadian economy is usually discussed in terms of national accounting concepts such as Gross National Product or Expenditure, or National Income, concepts which are often vaguely understood by even the best informed laymen. This is partly explicable on grounds of their quite recent origin. First estimates of National Income in Canada appeared in 1919 and the main feature of the present system of Canadian National Accounts were worked out in collaboration with British and American experts—whose governments were advancing along the same line—in meetings in September, 1944. The present diagrams, with lines radiating out like the spokes of a wheel and arrows indicating certain channels through which money flows in and out of the national economy, are attempts to illustrate a few basic definitions. A comparison of the 1931 and 1956 diagrams (the latter scaled down to allow for the decline in the value of the dollar) shows at a glance the striking growth of the economy as a whole in the last quarter-century.

Detailed study of the larger diagram should begin with the line marked Gross National Expenditure and proceed clockwise around the wheel—keeping in mind however that for the sake of simplicity only approximate figures are given and some smaller factors in the system have been omitted altogether. The Gross National Expenditure, it will be noted, is the largest spoke and represents therefore the largest amount, $30 billion. Without pausing to examine the meaning of Gross National Expenditure for the moment, the next facts shown are that some $4 billion are drawn off by government in the form of Net Indirect Taxes while another $3 billion is assumed set aside for Capital Consumption Allowances or what is more familiarly known as depreciation. The remaining $23 billion is said to constitute the National Income. Part of this income, however, will not be paid out to persons but will be used for such purposes as adding to existing capital or paying corporation taxes. On the other hand, National Income is supplemented by Transfer Payments from

governments—money that governments have collected but do not spend themselves for goods or services, and instead 'transfer' back to individuals in such forms as family allowances and unemployment insurance benefits. National Income reduced by Earnings Not Paid Out and supplemented by Transfer Payments makes up the total Personal Income of Canadians—wages, business profits, pensions, and so on. Deduct Personal Savings and Personal Direct Taxes and what is left is Personal Expenditure. Completing the circle, it can now be seen that Personal Expenditure and Government Expenditure together with an amount for Business Fixed Capital Formation constitute Gross National Expenditure. Business Fixed Capital formation is made possible by drawing on parts of the Capital Consumption Allowances, Earnings Not Paid Out, Personal Savings, and also Foreign Investments. Foreign Investments usually bring into the economy an amount approximately equal to the amount taken from it to pay for the excess of Imports over Exports.

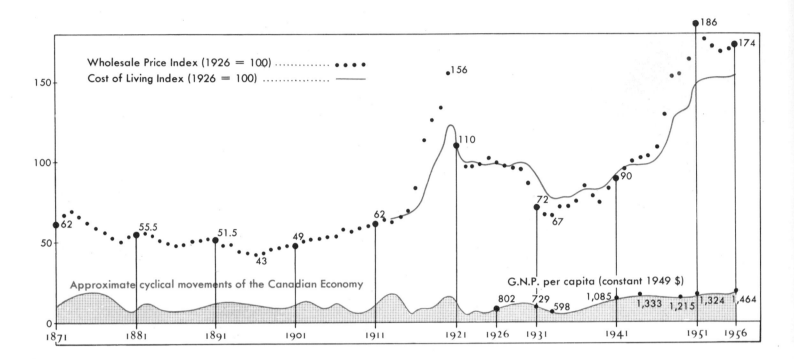

125　The Value of the Dollar

The fact that the dollar will buy less today than it would before the Second World War and considerably less than before the First World War is well known. This must be taken into account in the following pages where comparisons are made between recent and earlier periods with regard to the value of production in agriculture, mining, manufacturing, and other branches of the economy. It would mean little, for example, to show that the value of the wheat crop more than trebled between 1941 and 1956 unless this were qualified by pointing out that meantime the value of the dollar had been cut in half. What must be done therefore is to inflate or deflate the dollar statistically and try to give it a 'constant' value throughout the period. Each diagram must make clear what values were in 'constant' dollars as well as in those of the current year.

In the calculation of 'constant' dollars, no method can give more than an approximation of the truth. Closer approximations have been achieved by recent refinements using Composite Retail Indexes. These compare the amounts of food, clothing, and so on

that dollars would purchase in 1949, which is taken as the base year, with the amounts of each they would purchase in, say, 1956. Averages have been worked out and the resulting comparison of the general purchasing power of the 1956 with the 1949 dollar is known as the 1956 Composite Retail Index number. Figures for Gross National Product (the same amount as the Gross National Expenditure) based on 'constant' 1949 dollars are shown beneath the last four columns of diagram 126.

There are other more or less accurate yardsticks of dollar values including the Cost of Living Index and its successor, after 1952, the Consumer Price Index. Most have the disadvantage for the historian of having been calculated only for quite recent years. Fortunately one, the Wholesale Price Index, has been worked out back to 1871. It has accordingly been used to calculate the 'constant' dollars shown in all of the following diagrams. When compared with the more refined Cost of Living Index, as in the above diagram, there are seen to be some discrepancies. However, the two lines have

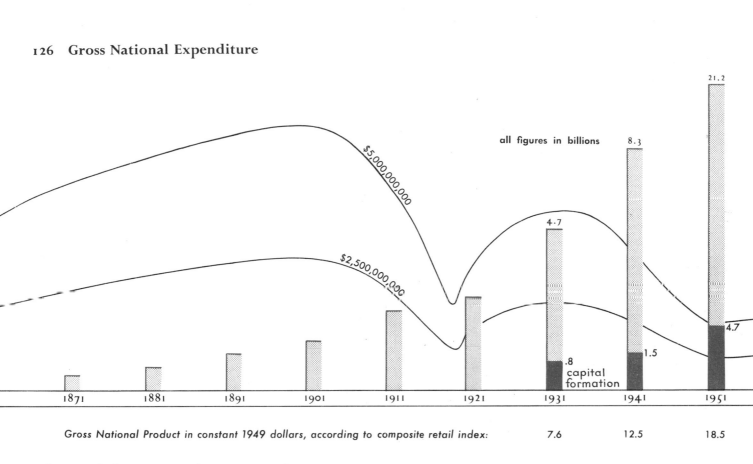

all figures in billions

Gross National Product in constant 1949 dollars, according to composite retail index: 7.6   12.5   18.5   23.6

at least much the same general contours and this must suffice for our purposes.

The technique used throughout is that used in the Gross National Expenditure diagram. The numbers at the top or along the side of each column represent actual or current dollars, and where no numbers are given there is no exact information available. The heights of the columns, on the other hand, are expanded or contracted to accord with the rise or fall in dollar values and indicate therefore 'constant' dollars. The $5 billion and the $2½ billion contour lines (omitted from subsequent diagrams to avoid clutter) make clear how this expansion and contraction is done. The lines themselves, based on the Wholesale Price Index, are in fact merely reciprocals of the Wholesale Price Index line in the facing diagram but with the irregularities of between-census years removed. That is, to the extent that the Wholesale Price Index line goes up, the dollar line goes down, and vice versa. One simple example of the significance of these lines can be seen by examining the $5 billion line where it passes just over the top of the

1931 column and similarly over the top of the Capital Formation section of the 1951 column. The amounts in each case are $4·7 billions, but the height which represents $4·7 billion in 1951 is less than half that representing the same amount in 1931 because the contour line and the dollar value it portrays have dropped so much in the meantime. Thus, to make a valid comparison of one period with another compare the heights of the columns; to find actual amounts in any one year in terms of that year's dollars, examine the figures.

While the Wholesale Price and Cost of Living Index diagram shows the rise and fall of dollar values, it also indicates by means of the wavy line at the bottom the successive periods of boom and depression that have occurred since 1871. This line is based on general estimates for the period before 1926 and from then on on the somewhat more accurate statistics available for Gross National Product.

The last four columns of the Gross National Expenditure diagram contain information, available only from 1931 on, regarding

total private and public capital formation. The total began to rise, proportionately to Gross National Expenditure, at a remarkable rate after the Second World War, reaching twice the level of that in the United States and becoming probably the highest in the world.

THE GROWTH OF THE ECONOMY

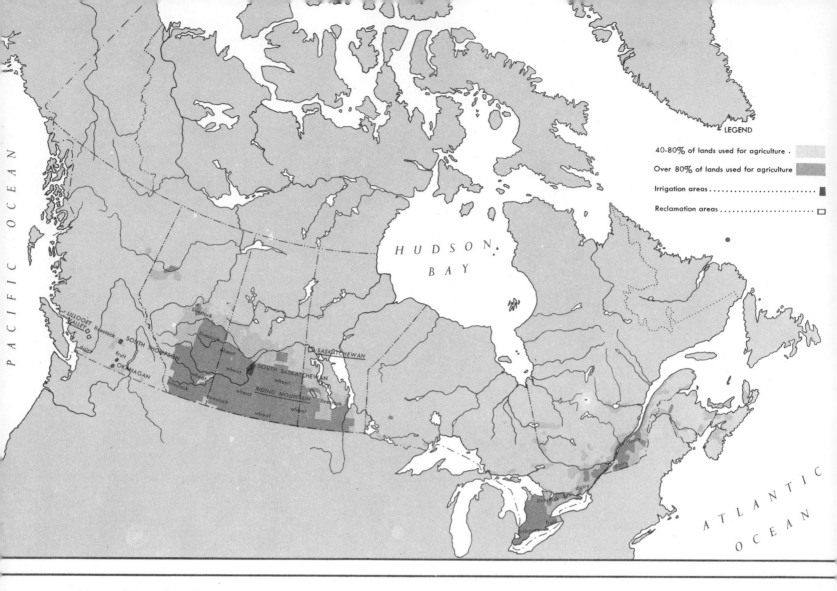

127 Map of Farming Areas

Developments that have transformed Canadian agriculture since Confederation include the spread of settlement across the continent, the growth of scientific knowledge, the increased use of machinery, and changes in export markets and in domestic eating habits. Some of the main features of this transformation are illustrated on these pages. The map shows areas of farm settlement before and since 1867, gives some information about the principal products, and draws attention to major recent and projected land-improvement undertakings. The diagrams supplement the map by showing the historical sequence and the extent of the changes in greater detail.

The lines on the Acreage and Production diagram make clear the rapid rise in acreage of both occupied and improved farm land in the period after 1901 when the West was being opened. A distinct slowing down followed 1931 with its drought and depression, and after 1941 old land was gradually abandoned at the same rate as new was occupied, although the total of improved land did continue to increase slightly. The two most striking features of this last period, however, are shown in the columns of this diagram and in the small separate diagram above it. They are that, despite the stability in acreage, total agricultural production went up at an accelerated rate while the total number of farms was going down.

These changes which were in many ways even more revolutionary than those connected with the period of westward expansion are not difficult to explain. They resulted from: (1) tremendously increased efficiency on the part of farm labour, made possible by the use of tractors and other farm machinery and appliances, some of which became available because of rural electrification; (2) the application of new scientific knowledge including, for example, the introduction of higher-yield and disease-resistant plants, chemical control of weeds, and better breeding procedures, especially the extensive use of artificial insemination; (3) improved marketing based on new methods of preparation such as cooling, freezing, and dehydrating, and more care in grading, packing, and delivery.

Many of these changes involved heavier capital expenditure. Farms that were too small or contained land that was too poor to afford this had to be abandoned or were absorbed by larger neighbours. The number of farms therefore declined steadily, as did the number of farm workers, the latter by an average of about 30,000 annually for some years after the Second World War. Nevertheless, the total value of farm production and the farmers' total gross income (both in terms of 'constant' dollars) rose at an unequalled rate between 1941 and 1951 and although they fell off slightly before 1956 they remained at a substantially higher level than in the pre-war period.

The columns in the Acreage and Production diagram draw attention to one other important trend of the mid-twentieth century—that is towards a reduced emphasis on field crops and instead some increase in dairying and a considerable increase in other production. This can be accounted for by the post-war difficulties in selling wheat abroad and by the rapid growth of Canada's own population and wealth. Both of these

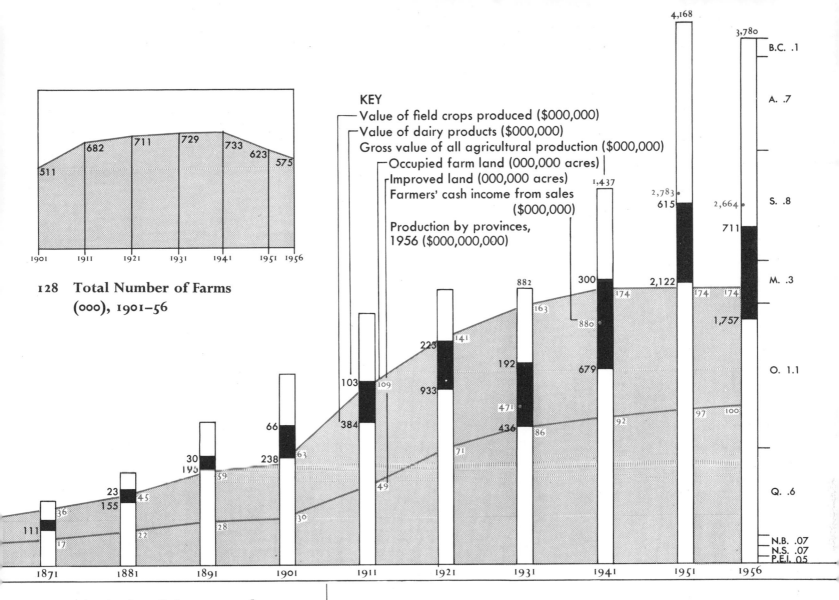

128 Total Number of Farms (000), 1901–56

KEY
Value of field crops produced ($000,000)
Value of dairy products ($000,000)
Gross value of all agricultural production ($000,000)
Occupied farm land (000,000 acres)
Improved land (000,000 acres)
Farmers' cash income from sales ($000,000)
Production by provinces, 1956 ($000,000,000)

129 Agricultural Acreage and Production

factors served to make the domestic market of proportionally greater importance. At the same time Canadian eating habits changed noticeably in the direction of reduced consumption of cereals and potatoes and greater use of dairy products, of high-protein foods such as meats, poultry, and eggs, and of fruits and vegetables.

Wheat remained nevertheless Canada's greatest single agricultural product. The diagram dealing with its production gives some idea of the fluctuations that have taken place in its price, yield, and even acreage since 1911 when it began some three decades of leadership among Canada's exports. These fluctuations constituted the greatest problem faced by Canadian agriculture in this period and had important effects on the Canadian economy as a whole.

130 Wheat Production, 1911–56

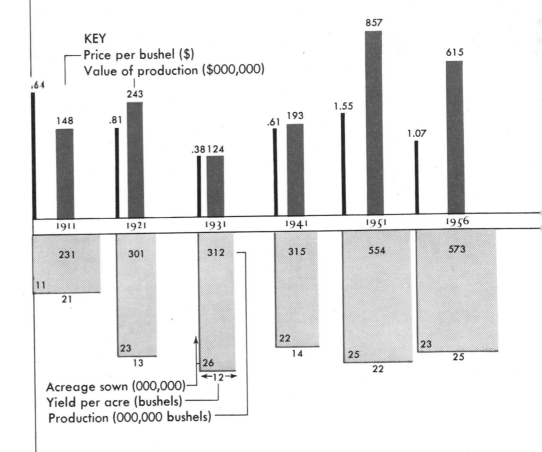

KEY
Price per bushel ($)
Value of production ($000,000)

Acreage sown (000,000)
Yield per acre (bushels)
Production (000,000 bushels)

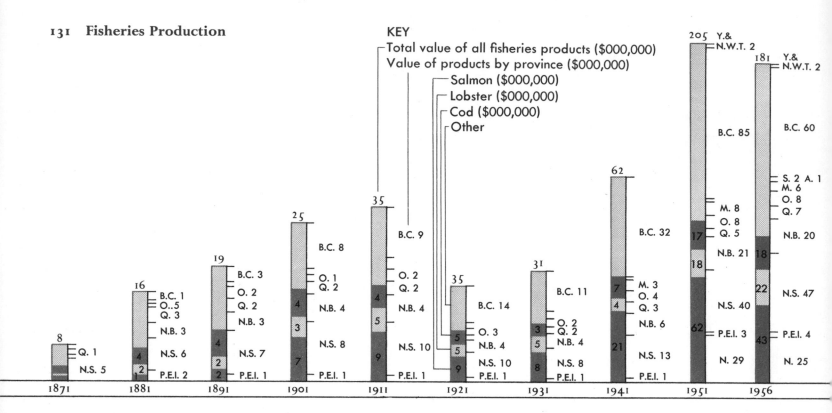

KEY

┌ Total value of all fisheries products ($000,000)
└ Value of products by province ($000,000)
  ┌ Salmon ($000,000)
  ├ Lobster ($000,000)
  ├ Cod ($000,000)
  └ Other

Long Atlantic and Pacific coastlines and inland lakes and rivers that contain over half the fresh water of the globe have made it possible for Canada's fisheries to become of major significance. Indeed by the mid-twentieth century Canada led the world in monetary returns from the export of fishery products. The diagram surveying this development has two special weaknesses: (1) fishery statistics are more than usually unreliable, especially for earlier decades; (2) remarkably great variations occur from year to year in both catch and price and the particular years shown here are not always typical in all respects of their decades. Nevertheless, taken in broad outline, the diagram does illustrate certain fundamental features of the industry.

The fisheries, like other branches of the Canadian economy but of earlier importance than most, advanced at a fairly steady pace until after the First World War. They dropped back in the highly competitive 1920's and 1930's, recovered again during the Second World War, and went on to new

heights in the years that followed, assisted by improved marketing techniques and changing North American dietary habits.

Cod, salmon, and lobster have long been the most important catches, with herring or halibut sometimes displacing one or the other in second or third position. Cod was the earliest to take the lead. It is found mainly on the east coast throughout the very broad continental shelf which includes the great fishing banks. Canadians, unlike the Newfoundlanders and others, caught it only inshore until 1873 when the first deep-sea vessels began to set out for the banks from Lunenburg. Salmon made rapid gains commercially, especially after canning began on the west coast about 1870, and by 1895 it was in first place where it has since remained by a substantial margin. Lobster, entirely an east-coast product, replaced cod in second position during the 1930's after having challenged its lead for several decades. Second World War austerities reduced its market, but by the 1950's it fully recovered its prewar place.

Until about 1918 the east-coast fisheries generally exceeded those of the west coast in total value of production. Then for some time they fell behind due mainly to the preeminence of British Columbia salmon. By the 1950's they were regaining their lead, even apart from the addition of Newfoundland's output after 1949. This was largely because of the continuing tremendous resources of the east coast, virtually undepleted through centuries of fishing, and to their exploitation by new techniques, many of them already familiar on the west coast and in the United States. The introduction of more efficient boats and nets made possible larger catches at lower costs. New methods of filleting and quick-freezing aided marketing. Even the problems facing the old and declining dry-fish trade could not prevent a strong upward trend in the industry as a whole. Meanwhile, the fresh-water fisheries, although unable to rival those of either the east or west coasts, had become important locally and were adding appreciably to national output.

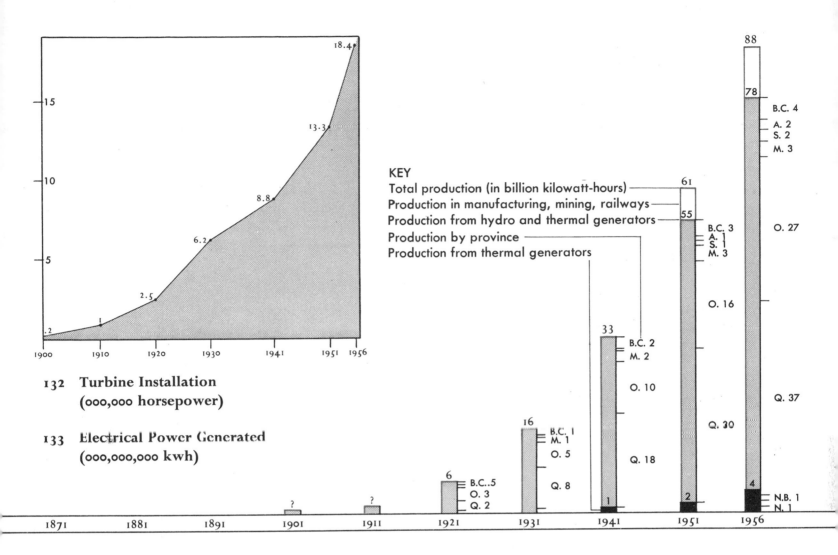

KEY

Total production (in billion kilowatt-hours)
Production in manufacturing, mining, railways
Production from hydro and thermal generators
Production by province
Production from thermal generators

132 Turbine Installation
(000,000 horsepower)

133 Electrical Power Generated
(000,000,000 kwh)

Electric power has been vital in the development of the pulp and paper, mining, and manufacturing industries dealt with in the following pages, as it has been in connection with many other aspects of modern life. Statistical information regarding it is somewhat scanty until recent decades and what there is is not uniform throughout. For example, before 1951 figures were not available distinguishing electrical production for their own use by manufacturing plants, mines, and railways, from production for sale by central electric stations. The general facts, however, are clear: with respect to power, and hydro-electric power in particular, Canada is one of the leading nations of the world; in installed water-turbine capacity she was by the mid-twentieth century second only to the United States.

The recent and very rapid hydro-electric development illustrated in the accompanying diagrams is undoubtedly one of the most significant features of Canada's economic progress. It may be given a somewhat exaggerated emphasis, however, unless the following qualifications are kept in mind: (1) there was power in substantial quantity before there was hydro-electric power—

nineteenth-century mills, machinery, and railways were run by steam or direct water or wind power; (2) coal is still used extensively as a source of energy, oil and natural gas are becoming increasingly important, and atomic power is just beginning. One example may be worth mentioning in this connection: liquid petroleum fuels are estimated to have supplied 9% of Canada's net energy consumption in 1926 and 37% in 1952—this despite the tremendous increase in hydro-electric power during the same period.

Use of electricity in Canada began to be of some significance late in the nineteenth century for such purposes as street lighting. What made large-scale expansion possible after 1900 was the introduction of high-tension methods of transmission over long distances eventually up to 300 miles. Growth followed at a steady but unspectacular rate until after the First World War when large new installations were undertaken. As these came into production between 1923 and 1935 hydro-electricity emerged as a major factor in the Canadian economy. The years after the depression of the 1930's saw little further progress, but when the Second World War broke out rapid advances became essential

and in the post-war period the pace became still faster.

As the map on the following page makes clear, Canada's developed and potential water-power resources are widespread though some in the north are too far from centres of population to be of use in the foreseeable future. Those of Ontario and Quebec, depending on the flow of the St. Lawrence and its great water system, have always been pre-eminent. However, resources within range of major industrial centres, especially in Ontario, have already been quite fully developed. Indeed Ontario's need for new power had become so critical by the end of the Second World War that her advocacy of the St. Lawrence Seaway and Power project, with special emphasis on its latter aspect, became insistent; and before the project was completed thermal plants had had to be built at Toronto and Windsor to meet immediate needs. Progress in British Columbia has been great in recent years and has included the very large Kitimat undertaking. In the Prairies and the Maritimes, the availability of coal has led to a blending of thermal and hydro development to a much greater extent than in other regions.

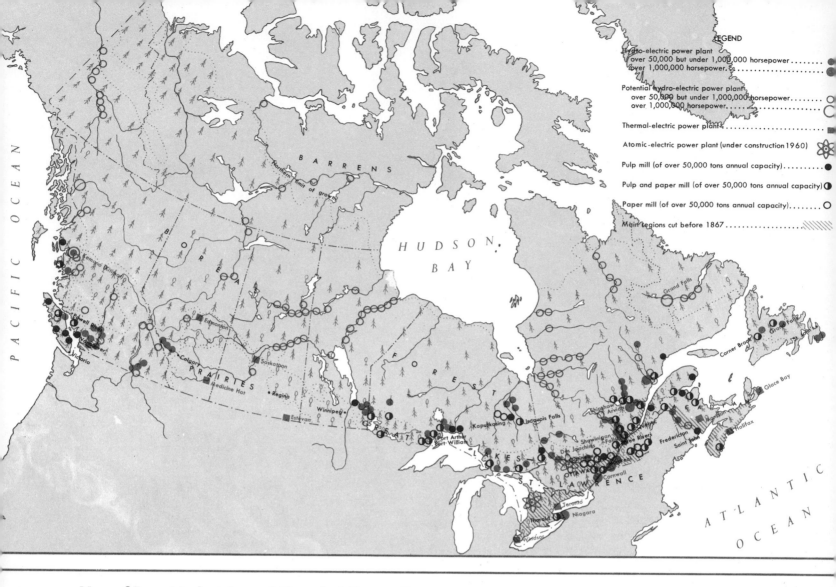

134 Map of Forest Industries and Electrical Power Sites

LEGEND

Hydro-electric power plant
over 50,000 but under 1,000,000 horsepower........
over 1,000,000 horsepower........................

Potential hydro-electric power plant
over 50,000 but under 1,000,000 horsepower........
over 1,000,000 horsepower.....................

Thermal-electric power plant.......................

Atomic-electric power plant (under construction 1960)

Pulp mill (of over 50,000 tons annual capacity).........

Pulp and paper mill (of over 50,000 tons annual capacity)

Paper mill (of over 50,000 tons annual capacity)........

Main regions cut before 1867...................

Planks and boards were Canada's leading export at the end of the nineteenth century; newsprint held that position in the mid-twentieth century and its production had become Canada's largest single manufacturing enterprise. These facts are indicative of the major importance of Canada's forest resources. The large-scale utilization of these resources was made possible by their great extent, as shown in the map, and by the ready availability of water transportation and power. Lack of authoritative statistics for all but recent years is unfortunate, though less so in regard to pulp and paper because that industry was very small before 1911. Lumbering, on the other hand, occupied a leading place throughout the nineteenth century. The export of square timber and 'deals' to Britain and later of planks and boards to the United States, together with the domestic use of timber for various purposes including shipbuilding, meant that total production was always very substantial indeed, although never quite as

high as early in the twentieth century.

Study of the diagram should begin by noting that successive columns in each annual set represent successive stages in production. That is, in the case of the upper columns relating to the pulp and paper industry, the first column gives the value of trees cut for pulpwood, the second, the value of the processed pulp, and the third, the value of the final product, paper. The lower columns show similarly first, the value of the trees cut for other than pulpwood, and second, the value of sawmill products. By adding the first columns, upper and lower, together, the total value of primary woods operations in the year can be found.

An important factor in the pulp and paper industry is the extent to which the products of the first and second stages are exported instead of being manufactured in Canada. The export of pulpwood is shown on the diagram by the small bar to the left of the pulpwood column. In 1941, for example, $16,000,000 out of $75,000,000 worth of

pulpwood was exported. The remainder, along with chips and scraps not included in the first column, was manufactured into some $175,000,000 worth of pulp. The gap beneath the next column shows that $86,000,000 worth of pulp was in turn exported. The rest became $241,000,000 worth of paper of which $159,000,000 worth was newsprint. The provincial distribution of paper production is shown in the usual way by bars on the right.

Sawmill operations are the most important dealt with in the lower columns. Beginning in 1941 when the necessary information became available the value of trees used in sawmills can be shown as a distinct part of each first column. The remainder of the column is made up of such items as wood cut for fuel, pit props, fence and telephone poles, and railway ties. The second column distinguishes similarly between lumber production and total sawmill production, the latter including shingles, laths, and so on, as well as lumber.

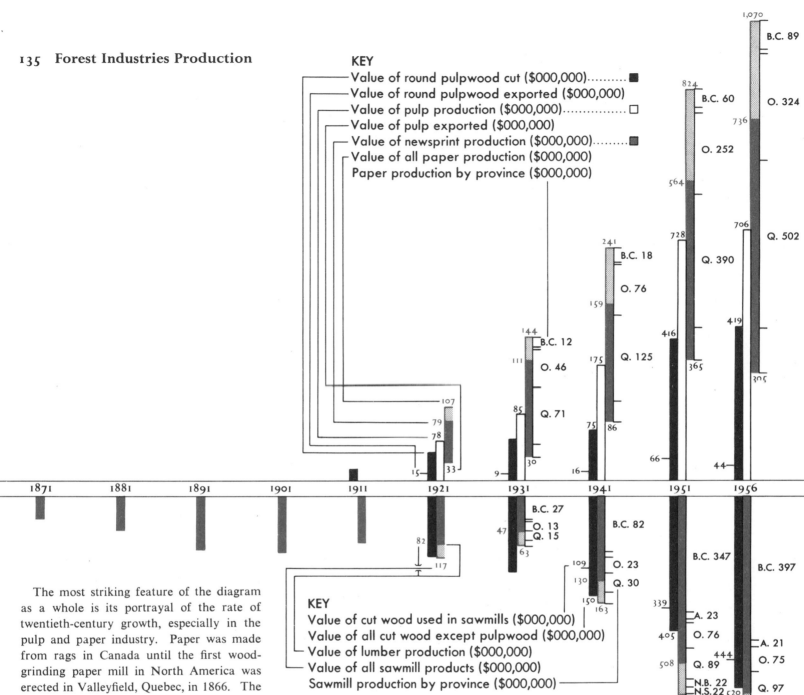

KEY
- Value of round pulpwood cut ($000,000).......... ■
- Value of round pulpwood exported ($000,000)
- Value of pulp production ($000,000)............... □
- Value of pulp exported ($000,000)
- Value of newsprint production ($000,000)........ ▨
- Value of all paper production ($000,000)
- Paper production by province ($000,000)

KEY
- Value of cut wood used in sawmills ($000,000)
- Value of all cut wood except pulpwood ($000,000)
- Value of lumber production ($000,000)
- Value of all sawmill products ($000,000)
- Sawmill production by province ($000,000)

The most striking feature of the diagram as a whole is its portrayal of the rate of twentieth-century growth, especially in the pulp and paper industry. Paper was made from rags in Canada until the first wood-grinding paper mill in North America was erected in Valleyfield, Quebec, in 1866. The first chemical pulp mill followed in 1869 at Windsor Mills, Quebec, and by 1900 pulp and paper output totalled some $8,000,000 a year. From then on production, especially of newsprint, increased with phenomenal rapidity. Throughout, Quebec with its great stands of spruce and balsam and huge water-power resources retained its early lead. British Columbia, on the other hand, emerged gradually as the great lumbering province, aided in this by the opening of the Panama Canal. In the years before the Second World War its production more than equalled that of the whole of eastern Canada. The war favoured the east temporarily, but in the post-war period British Columbia's lead continued to grow.

THE GROWTH OF THE ECONOMY

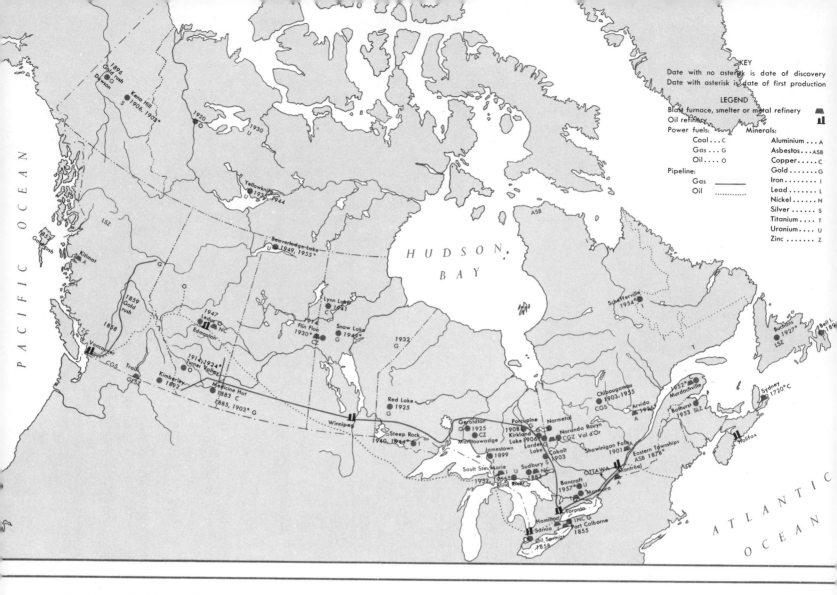

Until the mid-twentieth century when Canadian mining suddenly surged ahead, its progress had been intermittent and of major significance only in a few areas and with respect to a few minerals. Before Confederation there had been the coal and gypsum production of Nova Scotia, the gold rush to British Columbia, and some small local enterprises elsewhere. The building of the Canadian Pacific Railway first tapped, in the 1880's and 1890's, important mining areas in the Pre-Cambrian Shield and the Cordilleras, notably the copper-nickel resources of Sudbury, the copper-gold of Rossland, and the silver-lead-zinc of the Sullivan Mine near Kimberley. Other railway building had similar results as time went on, particularly in the case of the Timiskaming and Northern Ontario (later the Ontario Northland) Railway which led to the spectacular silver discoveries of the Cobalt region and eventually the opening up of the

entire Porcupine-Kirkland Lake area. The railways themselves, and steamships, constituted a whole new market for coal from the old mines of Nova Scotia and from new ones developed in Alberta and British Columbia. Beginning in the 1920's the aeroplane became the key to a further stage in the expansion of the mining frontier. Air prospecting and transportation and later the use of the aeroplane for geophysical surveying made the resources of the whole of northern Canada accessible.

Research, development, and marketing are as important as discovery for mining progress. The Sullivan Mine, for example, was known as early as 1892, but became a major producer only after a new electrolytic process for separating lead and zinc was introduced at the Trail smelter in 1916. Similarly the nickel-copper areas of Sudbury, although discovered in 1883, had to await significant development until after 1900 and further

much larger exploitation until the enormous markets of the period after the Second World War came into existence. In this latter period other old properties as well, along with many new ones, underwent extraordinary advances due to a combination of favourable circumstances—fresh discoveries, improved techniques, growing American shortages, high prices, and abundant capital, particularly from the United States. This was true in connection with minerals of which Canada had already for some time been a leading world producer such as gold, copper, nickel, lead, zinc, and asbestos. It was true also of the post-war additions to Canada's large-scale production, oil, iron, and uranium. The oil strike at Leduc in 1947, dwarfing earlier Turner Valley finds, initiated huge growth throughout Alberta and adjacent regions, including eventually the construction of oil and gas pipelines to markets in other parts of the United States and Canada. Iron

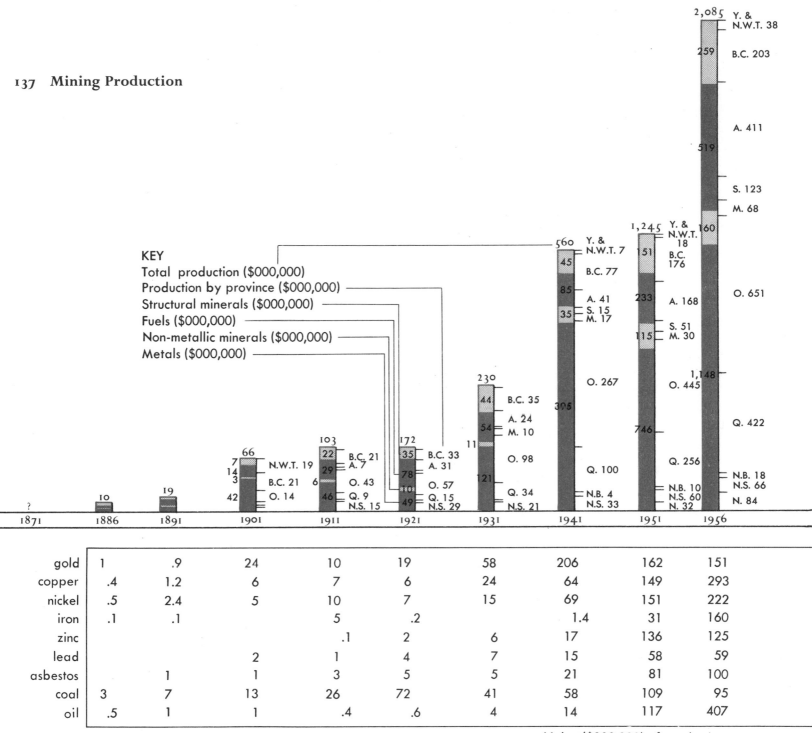

KEY
Total production ($000,000)
Production by province ($000,000)
Structural minerals ($000,000)
Fuels ($000,000)
Non-metallic minerals ($000,000)
Metals ($000,000)

	1871	1886	1891	1901	1911	1921	1931	1941	1951	1956
gold	1	.9	24	10	19	58	206	162	151	
copper	.4	1.2	6	7	6	24	64	149	293	
nickel	.5	2.4	5	10	7	15	69	151	222	
iron	.1	.1		5	.2		1.4	31	160	
zinc				.1	2	6	17	136	125	
lead			2	1	4	7	15	58	59	
asbestos		1	1	3	5	5	21	81	100	
coal	3	7	13	26	72	41	58	109	95	
oil	.5	1	1	.4	.6	4	14	117	407	

Value ($000,000) of production

138 Production of Selected Minerals

ore at Steep Rock and on the Quebec-Labrador boundary, developed at great capital cost when the Mesabi Range in the United States was approaching exhaustion, suddenly became another of Canada's leading mineral products. Only less significant were the uranium mines of the Beaverlodge area of Saskatchewan and of Blind River in Ontario. Not so important individually, but bulking large in total, were increases in production of a wide variety of other minerals used in industry and construction. Coal, on the other hand, because of the new competition from oil, tended to fall off in relative importance.

THE GROWTH OF THE ECONOMY

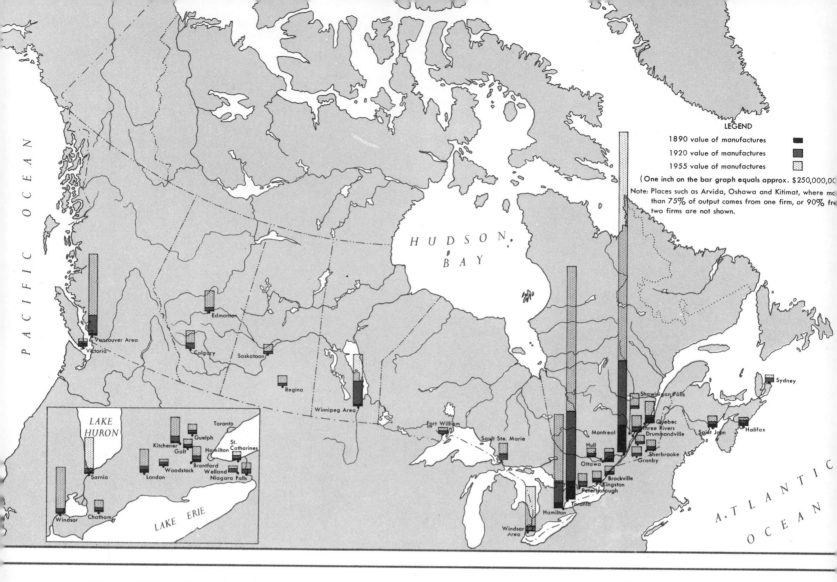

139 Map of Manufacturing Areas

By the mid-twentieth century, Canada stood about sixth among the nations of the world with respect to manufacturing. At Confederation and for many years afterwards she had been known instead for her primary products. The general nature of the manufacturing growth which brought about this remarkable change is shown on the accompanying map and diagram, although as usual the statistics on which they are based contain inconsistencies. These cause difficulties particularly in trying to compare figures for before and after 1917, when the present annual Census of Manufactures was commenced using a new method of analysis; and even after 1917 there has not been complete uniformity. Only since 1924, for example, have figures for the net value of manufactured products been obtained by subtracting from gross values the costs of materials and fuel and also of electricity. Before that time costs of electricity were not subtracted or even recorded separately in a way that would make comparisons possible.

Nevertheless, the general facts are evident. At Confederation, Canadian manufacturing was mainly of the domestic or village sort, concerned with products needed locally and capable of being manufactured for the most part from local resources. Leading examples include flour, cheese, butter, meats, timber and articles made from it, leather goods, textiles, and some iron and steel products. Wooden shipbuilding, in a class by itself, was just passing its peak. The succeeding decades, to the end of the nineteenth century, were disappointing, although less so in manufacturing than in some other branches of the economy. The extensive railway building and the tariff protection offered after 1879 in accordance with Macdonald's 'National Policy' helped manufacturing weather reasonably well the generally depressed conditions of the time. Real expansion could come, however, only with the opening of the West and the consequent enlarging of the domestic market; and just when this was getting well under way the pace was further accelerated by the outbreak of the First World War with its great demands on the shipbuilding and steel industries and many others, notably non-ferrous metal refining. The brief post-war collapse of 1921 was followed by renewed progress especially in the pulp and paper industry and then by the long depression of the 1930's. War again, after 1939, stimulated rapid additions to manufacturing capacity, this time on a far larger scale than in the previous generation. Most striking were developments in such fields as the non-ferrous metals, tool-making, electrical apparatus, and chemicals. When peace came much of the new capacity was found adaptable to peacetime uses. And finally, in the 1950's Canadian manufacturing rose to unprecedented heights as a result of the discovery of huge new resources, particularly of gas, oil, iron ore, and other important minerals, and their development with the assistance of American capital and under pressure from the Korean War and subsequent tension with Russia.

Provincial distribution of manufacturing, as the map and diagram show, has been most uneven ever since the period of modern expansion began. Ontario has consistently maintained the lead, followed by Quebec and,

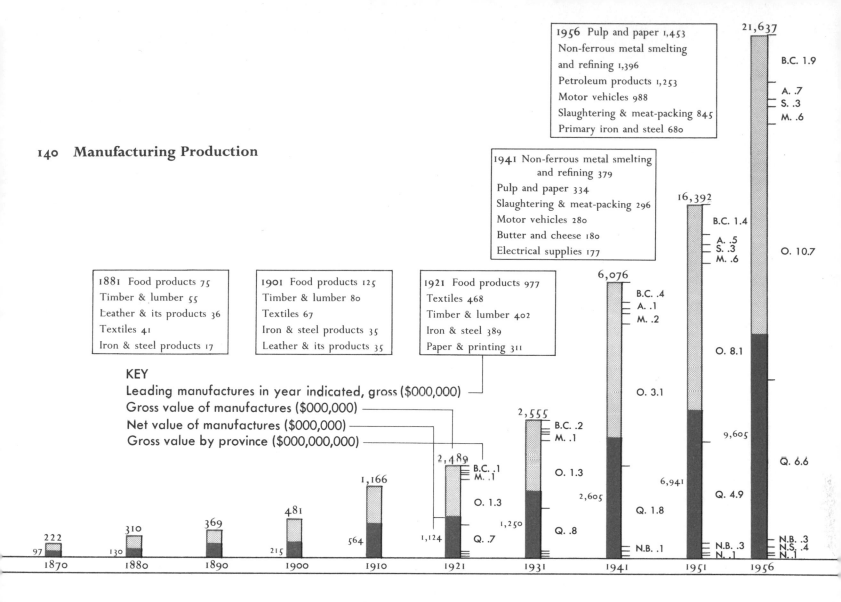

1956 Pulp and paper 1,453
Non-ferrous metal smelting
and refining 1,396
Petroleum products 1,253
Motor vehicles 988
Slaughtering & meat-packing 845
Primary iron and steel 680

21,637
B.C. 1.9
A. .7
S. .3
M. .6

1941 Non-ferrous metal smelting
and refining 379
Pulp and paper 334
Slaughtering & meat-packing 296
Motor vehicles 280
Butter and cheese 180
Electrical supplies 177

16,392
B.C. 1.4
A. .5
S. .3
M. .6
O. 10.7

1881 Food products 75
Timber & lumber 55
Leather & its products 36
Textiles 41
Iron & steel products 17

1901 Food products 125
Timber & lumber 80
Textiles 67
Iron & steel products 35
Leather & its products 35

1921 Food products 977
Textiles 468
Timber & lumber 402
Iron & steel 389
Paper & printing 311

KEY
Leading manufactures in year indicated, gross ($000,000)
Gross value of manufactures ($000,000)
Net value of manufactures ($000,000)
Gross value by province ($000,000,000)

6,076
B.C. .4
A. .1
M. .2
O. 3.1

9,605

Q. 4.9

Q. 6.6

2,555
B.C. .2
M. .1
O. 1.3
Q. .8

2,489
B.C. .1
M. .1
O. 1.3
Q. .7

6,941
Q. 1.8
N.B. .1

2,605

1,250

1,166

564

481

215

369

310

222

97

130

1,124

N.B. .3
N. .1

N.B. .3
N.S. .4
N. .1

1870 1880 1890 1900 1910 1921 1931 1941 1951 1956

---

at a considerable distance, by British Columbia. The transportation and power facilities of the St. Lawrence region have clearly made inevitable the large concentration of industry there. Only a few other places with very special advantages have emerged as significant at all—Winnipeg, 'the gateway to the West', Edmonton and Calgary with their developing gas and oil supplies, and Vancouver on the rapidly advancing Pacific coast with its great Cordilleran power and mineral resources.

Lack of space makes it possible only to mention other quite important changes in manufacturing since Confederation — the trend from small to larger establishments with very much larger capital investment, the improved methods and equipment and the resulting increases in per capita output despite reduced hours of work, and the relative decline in the food, textile, and lumbering industries as compared with others such as pulp and paper, iron, non-ferrous metals, and chemicals.

Transportation and Communications

Transportation and communications have always been of special importance in Canada with its great distances and widely dispersed population. They have accordingly received full attention in the earlier sections of this atlas in maps ranging from the period of the fur-trade routes to that of the railways and the St. Lawrence canals. The diagrams on the following two pages supplement those maps with important statistical information. Communications: Telegraphic communications in Canada date back to the opening of a Toronto–Hamilton line in 1846. Before Confederation main centres had been linked with each other and with American lines in both Canada and the Maritimes and an Atlantic cable had come into operation. The growth of telegraph mileage has followed a similar pattern to that of railway mileage, as can be seen on the Communications and Railway diagrams—a natural

development in view of the close association of these two services. The recent decline in telegraph mileage gives a misleading impression. It is the result of more efficient organization and methods and the number of messages sent has continued to rise far above earlier levels. The telephone patented by Alexander Graham Bell in 1876 came into use slowly until the beginning of the twentieth century. Then with increasing rapidity it became a major factor in transforming business and personal means of communication.

Railways: The Railways diagram reinforces what has been said earlier about the great period of railway construction between Confederation and the First World War. The subsequent levelling off in mileage was only slightly affected by the extension of lines in the 1950's to the new mineral centres. The amount of freight carried declined in the depression years of the early 1930's, but went up again rapidly during the periods of war and post-war economic expansion.

THE GROWTH OF THE ECONOMY

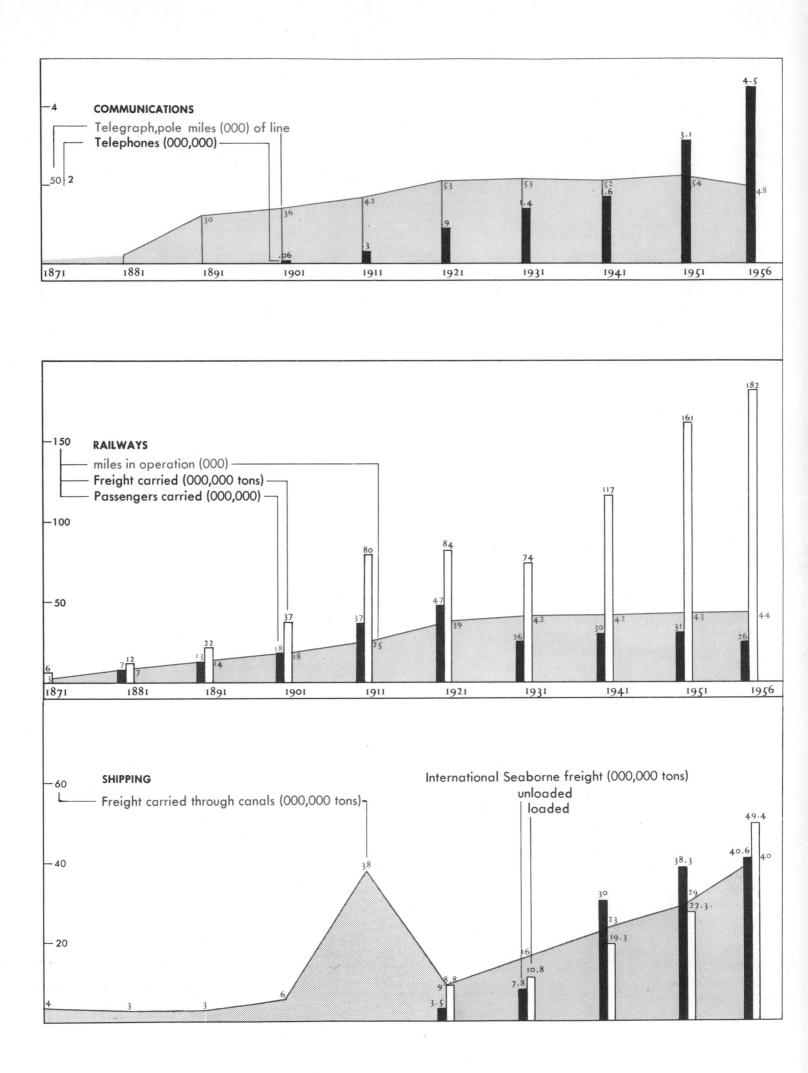

COMMUNICATIONS

Telegraph, pole miles (000) of line
Telephones (000,000)

		30	36	4.2	53	53	52 .6	3.1 54

4.5
4.8

.06 | 3 | 9 | 1.4

1871 · 1881 · 1891 · 1901 · 1911 · 1921 · 1931 · 1941 · 1951 · 1956

RAILWAYS

miles in operation (000)
Freight carried (000,000 tons)
Passengers carried (000,000)

182
161
117
80 · 84 · 74
47
6 7 12 13 22 18 37 37 39 26 42 30 42 31 43 26 44
3 7 14 18 25

1871 · 1881 · 1891 · 1901 · 1911 · 1921 · 1931 · 1941 · 1951 · 1956

SHIPPING

Freight carried through canals (000,000 tons)

International Seaborne freight (000,000 tons)
unloaded
loaded

38
49.4
40.6 40
38.3
30
29
27.3
23
19.3
16
10.8
8.8
7.8
9
4 3 3 6 3.5

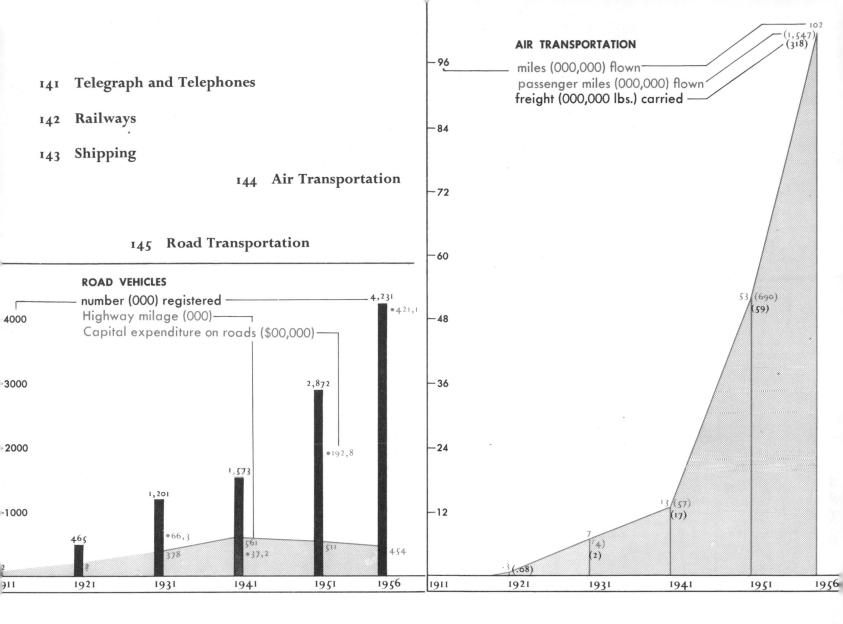

ROAD VEHICLES

number (000) registered ——————
Highway milage (000)——————
Capital expenditure on roads ($00,000)——————

AIR TRANSPORTATION

miles (000,000) flown——————
passenger miles (000,000) flown——————
freight (000,000 lbs.) carried——————

Transportation and Communications

(continued from page 103)

Passenger traffic was harder hit by road and air competition following the peak years of the 1920's. The effect of the automobile in particular in drawing off short-run traffic can be judged by the fact that while the drop in the number of passengers, as shown in the diagram, was very great indeed between 1921 and 1956, the drop in railway passenger miles was only from 2,960,000,000 to 2,907,000,000.

Shipping: Canadian canals are among the busiest in the world in spite of winter freeze-ups. The extraordinary amount of freight carried through them in the years around 1911 consisted mainly of large iron ore, coal, and grain shipments through the Sault Ste. Marie canal, most of them in American vessels. The improvements and greater use of the American locks at the Sault and also a post-war depression in the steel industry account for the sudden decline. Canada's seaborne trade was already important by the

time of Confederation, and has continued to grow. Figures for freight loading and unloading are not available for the period before 1921.

Road Transportation: The great rise in the number of road vehicles and in capital expenditure on roads especially after the Second World War is a well-known feature of modern transportation developments. The diagram's apparent indication of a decline in highway construction in recent years is due to a reclassification of roads in some provinces in a more realistic manner—the removal from the total, for example, of 'road allowances' through completely unopened country. Urban streets, not included in the diagram, amounted in 1956 to another 11,000 miles of hard-surfaced road, 9,000 miles of gravel, and 2,000 miles of dirt.

Air Transportation: Flying began in Canada in 1909 when J. A. D. McCurdy piloted the *Silver Dart* during a short flight at

Baddeck, Nova Scotia. After the First World War flying gradually became common, and 'bush' pilots began to play an increasing role in the opening of parts of the north country. It was not until 1930, however, that regularly scheduled air services began and from then on, as the diagram shows, revenue miles flown rose at a spectacular rate. After 1956 there was a levelling off, the figures for 1958 being some 100,000,000 miles, broken down as follows: by Canadian aircraft, 49,000,000 on domestic scheduled flights and 23,000,000 on non-scheduled, 8,000,000 to the United States, and 15,000,000 trans-ocean; and by foreign aircraft, 2,000,000 to the United States and 2,000,000 trans-ocean.

THE GROWTH OF THE ECONOMY

From the earliest days when fur was the export staple, Canada's foreign trade was extraordinarily large in proportion to the size of her economy as a whole. In keeping with this trend, Canada in 1956 ranked fourth among the nations of the world in the total amount of her foreign trade, and first on a per capita basis. As could be expected in a developing economy, imports exceeded exports except in unusual circumstances such as war years. Both grew substantially after the Second World War.

Although the trading pattern changed in some particulars over the decades, it remained on the whole relatively stable. The United Kingdom and the United States were always Canada's principal trading partners, but the latter had forged far ahead by the mid-twentieth century. Major exports were as a rule products of the forest and field, changing somewhat in order of importance with the passing of the years; major imports were manufactured goods apart from a few special requirements such as coal.

The deficit normal in Canada's foreign trade has usually been due to an excess of merchandise imported over that exported, and to such 'invisible' items as shipping charges, interest payments, tourist expenditure, and so on. It is compensated for mainly by direct foreign investment in Canadian enterprises and by foreign buying of Canadian Government and other securities. In 1941 and other war years the export of war materials especially to the United Kingdom created a temporary credit balance and there have been a few other occasions as well when for one reason or another the balance of payments has been in Canada's favour.

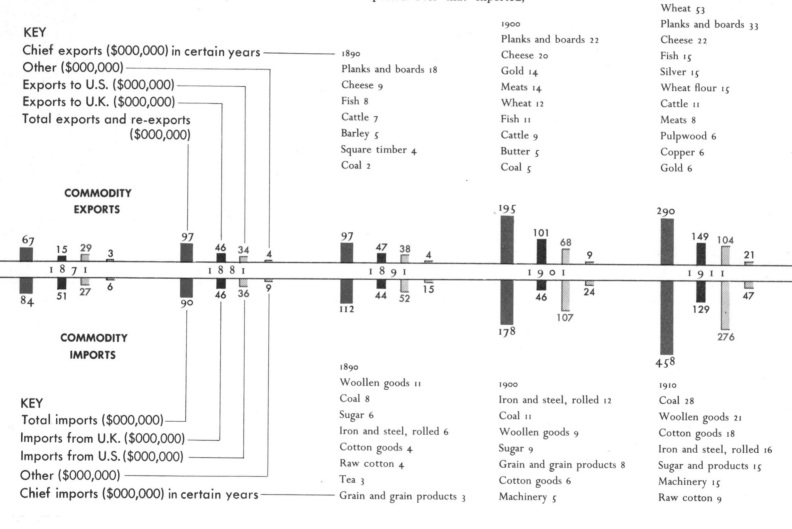

KEY

Chief exports ($000,000) in certain years
Other ($000,000)
Exports to U.S. ($000,000)
Exports to U.K. ($000,000)
Total exports and re-exports ($000,000)

COMMODITY EXPORTS

COMMODITY IMPORTS

KEY

Total imports ($000,000)
Imports from U.K. ($000,000)
Imports from U.S. ($000,000)
Other ($000,000)
Chief imports ($000,000) in certain years

1890
Planks and boards 18
Cheese 9
Fish 8
Cattle 7
Barley 5
Square timber 4
Coal 2

1900
Planks and boards 22
Cheese 20
Gold 14
Meats 14
Wheat 12
Fish 11
Cattle 9
Butter 5
Coal 5

1910
Wheat 53
Planks and boards 33
Cheese 22
Fish 15
Silver 15
Wheat flour 15
Cattle 11
Meats 8
Pulpwood 6
Copper 6
Gold 6

1890
Woollen goods 11
Coal 8
Sugar 6
Iron and steel, rolled 6
Cotton goods 4
Raw cotton 4
Tea 3
Grain and grain products 3

1900
Iron and steel, rolled 12
Coal 11
Woollen goods 9
Sugar 9
Grain and grain products 8
Cotton goods 6
Machinery 5

1910
Coal 28
Woollen goods 21
Cotton goods 18
Iron and steel, rolled 16
Sugar and products 15
Machinery 15
Raw cotton 9

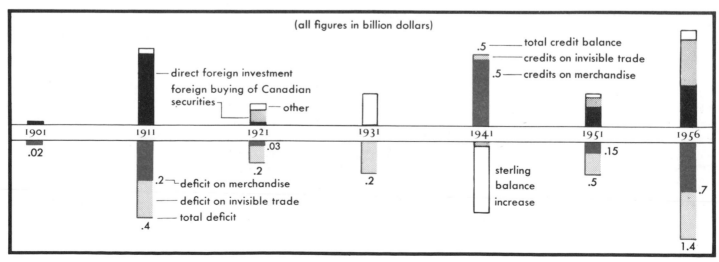

(all figures in billion dollars)

total credit balance
credits on invisible trade
credits on merchandise

direct foreign investment
foreign buying of Canadian securities
other

deficit on merchandise
deficit on invisible trade
total deficit

sterling balance increase

1901 .02
1911 .2 / .4
1921 .03 / .2
1931 .2
1941 .5 / .5
1951 .15 / .5
1956 .7 / 1.4

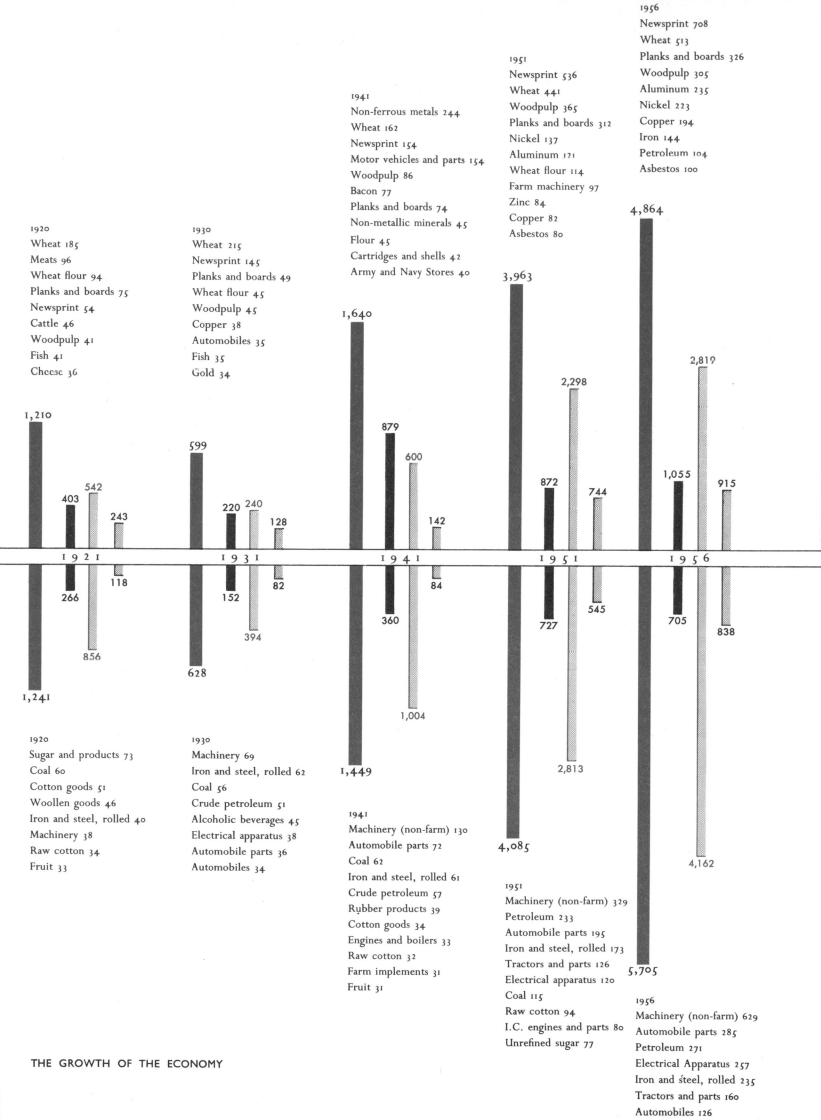

1956
Newsprint 708
Wheat 513
Planks and boards 326
Woodpulp 305
Aluminum 235
Nickel 223
Copper 194
Iron 144
Petroleum 104
Asbestos 100

1951
Newsprint 536
Wheat 441
Woodpulp 365
Planks and boards 312
Nickel 137
Aluminum 121
Wheat flour 114
Farm machinery 97
Zinc 84
Copper 82
Asbestos 80

1941
Non-ferrous metals 244
Wheat 162
Newsprint 154
Motor vehicles and parts 154
Woodpulp 86
Bacon 77
Planks and boards 74
Non-metallic minerals 45
Flour 45
Cartridges and shells 42
Army and Navy Stores 40

1920
Wheat 185
Meats 96
Wheat flour 94
Planks and boards 75
Newsprint 54
Cattle 46
Woodpulp 41
Fish 41
Cheese 36

1930
Wheat 215
Newsprint 145
Planks and boards 49
Wheat flour 45
Woodpulp 45
Copper 38
Automobiles 35
Fish 35
Gold 34

1,210
403
542
243
1921
266
118
856
1,241

599
220 240
128
1931
152
82
394
628

1,640
879
600
142
1941
360
84
1,004
1,449

3,963
872
2,298
744
1951
727
545
2,813
4,085

4,864
1,055
2,819
915
1956
705
838
4,162
5,705

1920
Sugar and products 73
Coal 60
Cotton goods 51
Woollen goods 46
Iron and steel, rolled 40
Machinery 38
Raw cotton 34
Fruit 33

1930
Machinery 69
Iron and steel, rolled 62
Coal 56
Crude petroleum 51
Alcoholic beverages 45
Electrical apparatus 38
Automobile parts 36
Automobiles 34

1941
Machinery (non-farm) 130
Automobile parts 72
Coal 62
Iron and steel, rolled 61
Crude petroleum 57
Rubber products 39
Cotton goods 34
Engines and boilers 33
Raw cotton 32
Farm implements 31
Fruit 31

1951
Machinery (non-farm) 329
Petroleum 233
Automobile parts 195
Iron and steel, rolled 173
Tractors and parts 126
Electrical apparatus 120
Coal 115
Raw cotton 94
I.C. engines and parts 80
Unrefined sugar 77

1956
Machinery (non-farm) 629
Automobile parts 285
Petroleum 271
Electrical Apparatus 257
Iron and steel, rolled 235
Tractors and parts 160
Automobiles 126
Pipes and tubes (iron and steel) 123

THE GROWTH OF THE ECONOMY

148   The Organization of Government

Canadian governmental organization with its executive, legislative, and judicial branches is outlined in the present diagram. The only major changes since Confederation are in the executive departments and an attempt has been made to show these as clearly and fully as possible, although for the sake of simplicity some details have had to be omitted.

The chart on the following pages which shows the result of all general elections since Confederation is self-explanatory.

MINISTRIES   showing date of formation.

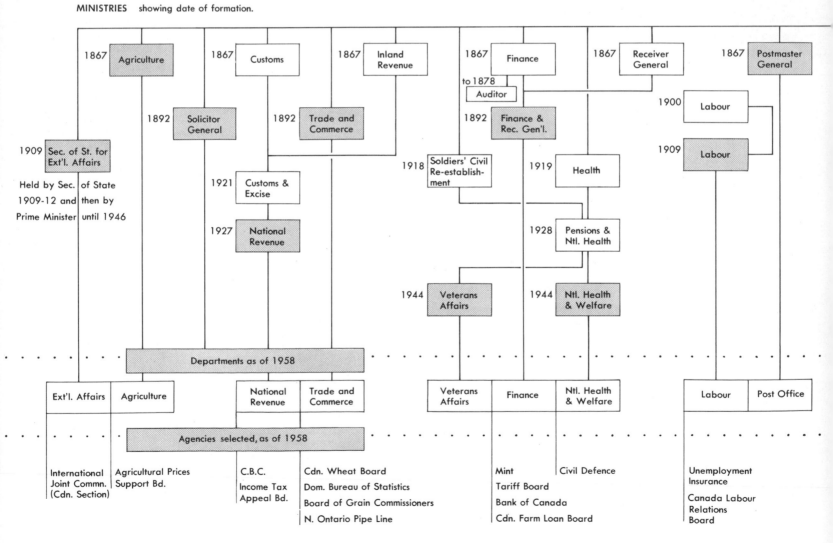

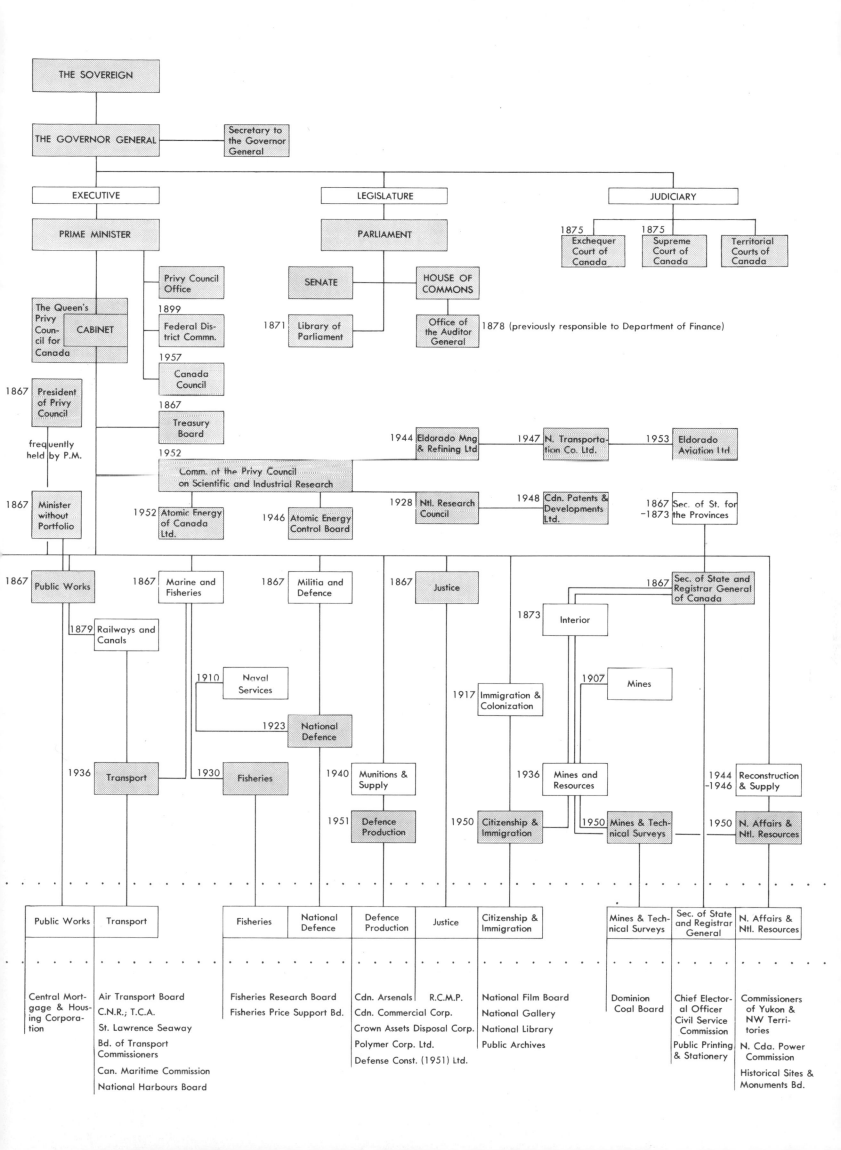

THE SOVEREIGN

THE GOVERNOR GENERAL — Secretary to the Governor General

EXECUTIVE | LEGISLATURE | JUDICIARY

PRIME MINISTER

PARLIAMENT

1875 Exchequer Court of Canada | 1875 Supreme Court of Canada | Territorial Courts of Canada

Privy Council Office

SENATE | HOUSE OF COMMONS

The Queen's Privy Council for Canada | CABINET

1899 Federal District Commn.

1871 Library of Parliament | Office of the Auditor General | 1878 (previously responsible to Department of Finance)

1957 Canada Council

1867 President of Privy Council

1867 Treasury Board

frequently held by P.M.

1952 Comm. of the Privy Council on Scientific and Industrial Research

1944 Eldorado Mng & Refining Ltd | 1947 N. Transportation Co. Ltd. | 1953 Eldorado Aviation Ltd.

1867 Minister without Portfolio

1952 Atomic Energy of Canada Ltd. | 1946 Atomic Energy Control Board

1928 Ntl. Research Council | 1948 Cdn. Patents & Developments Ltd. | 1867 –1873 Sec. of St. for the Provinces

1867 Public Works | 1867 Marine and Fisheries | 1867 Militia and Defence | 1867 Justice | 1867 Sec. of State and Registrar General of Canada

1873 Interior

1879 Railways and Canals

1910 Naval Services

1907 Mines

1917 Immigration & Colonization

1923 National Defence

1936 Transport | 1930 Fisheries | 1940 Munitions & Supply | 1936 Mines and Resources | 1944 –1946 Reconstruction & Supply

1951 Defence Production | 1950 Citizenship & Immigration | 1950 Mines & Technical Surveys | 1950 N. Affairs & Ntl. Resources

Public Works | Transport | Fisheries | National Defence | Defence Production | Justice | Citizenship & Immigration | Mines & Technical Surveys | Sec. of State and Registrar General | N. Affairs & Ntl. Resources

Central Mortgage & Housing Corporation | Air Transport Board
C.N.R.; T.C.A.
St. Lawrence Seaway
Bd. of Transport Commissioners
Can. Maritime Commission
National Harbours Board | Fisheries Research Board
Fisheries Price Support Bd. | Cdn. Arsenals
Cdn. Commercial Corp.
Crown Assets Disposal Corp.
Polymer Corp. Ltd.
Defense Const. (1951) Ltd. | R.C.M.P. | National Film Board
National Gallery
National Library
Public Archives | Dominion Coal Board | Chief Electoral Officer
Civil Service Commission
Public Printing & Stationery | Commissioners of Yukon & NW Territories
N. Cda. Power Commission
Historical Sites & Monuments Bd.

1867

1872

1874

1878

1882

1887

1891

1896

1900

1904

1908

1911

1917

1921

1925

1926

1930

1935

1940

1945

1949

1953

1957

1958

149 **Results of Federal General Elections**

110

POLITICAL TRENDS

4 8 12 Manitoba	4 8 12 16 Saskatchewan	4 8 12 16 Alberta	4 8 12 16 B.C.	Yukon (1902) & N.W. Territories	20 40 60 80 120 160 200 Total Seats	Prime Ministers	Governors General
					Liberals 80		
					Conservatives 101	1867 Sir John A. Macdonald	1867 VISCOUNT MONCK
							1868 BARON LISGAR
					97		
					103	1873 Alexander Mackenzie	1872 MARQUIS OF DUFFERIN
					133		
					73		
					69		
					137	1878 Sir John A. Macdonald	1878 MARQUIS OF LORNE
	4 8 12 N.W. Territories				71		
					139		1883 MARQUIS OF LANSDOWNE
					92		
					123		1888 BARON STANLEY
					92	1891 Sir John Abbott	
					123	1892 Sir John Thompson	1893 MARQUIS OF ABERDEEN
						1894 Sir Mackenzie Bowell	
					117	1896 Sir Charles Tupper	
					89	1896 Sir Wilfrid Laurier	
					Independents and Others 7		1898 EARL OF MINTO
					128		
					78		
					8		
					139	1901	1904 EARL GREY
					75	KING EDWARD VII	
					133		
					85		
					3	1910	
					86	1911 Sir Robert Borden	1911 DUKE OF CONNAUGHT
					132		
					3		
					Unionists 82		1916 DUKE OF DEVONSHIRE
					153	1920 Arthur Meighen	
					117	1921 W. L. Mackenzie King	
					Liberal-Conservatives 50		1921 VISCOUNT BYNG
					Progressives 64		
					4		
					101		
					Conservatives 116	1926 Arthur Meighen	
					24		
					4		1926 MARQUIS OF WILLINGDON
					116	1926 W. L. Mackenzie King	
					91		
					13		
					9		
					Liberal Progressives 11		
					United Farmers 5		
					88		
					137	1930 R. B. Bennett	
					2		
					3		1931 EARL OF BESSBOROUGH
					10		
					5		
					171	1935 W. L. Mackenzie King	
					39		1935 BARON TWEEDSMUIR
					C.C.F. 7	1936 K.ED. VIII	
					Social Credit 17	1936	
					11		
					178		
					39		1940 EARL OF ATHLONE
					8		
					10		
					10		
					125	1948 L. S. St.Laurent	
					67		
					28		1945 VISCOUNT ALEXANDER
					13		
					12		
					190		
					Progressive Conservatives 41		
					13		
					10		
					8		1952 VINCENT MASSEY
					170		
					51		
					23		
					15		
					6		
					105	1957 John G. Diefenbaker	
					112		
					25		
					19		
					4		
					208 48		1959 G. P. VANIER
					8		
					1		

(Vertical label on right panel: QUEEN VICTORIA / KING EDWARD VII / KING GEORGE V / KING GEORGE VI / QUEEN ELIZABETH II)

POLITICAL TRENDS

III

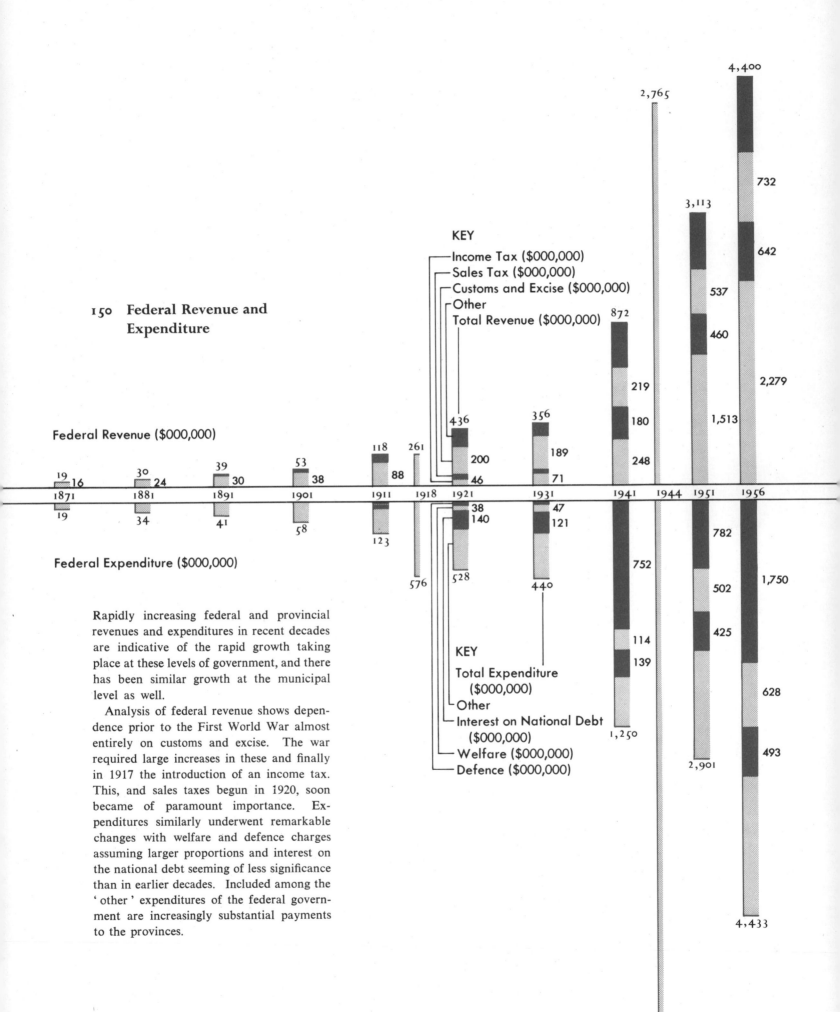

150 **Federal Revenue and Expenditure**

KEY

— Income Tax ($000,000)
— Sales Tax ($000,000)
— Customs and Excise ($000,000)
— Other
Total Revenue ($000,000)

Federal Revenue ($000,000)

19 16	30 24	39 30	53 38	118 88	261	436	356	872	2,765	3,113	4,400	

1871   1881   1891   1901   1911   1918   1921   1931   1941   1944   1951   1956

KEY

Total Expenditure
($000,000)
— Other
— Interest on National Debt
($000,000)
— Welfare ($000,000)
— Defence ($000,000)

Federal Expenditure ($000,000)

Rapidly increasing federal and provincial revenues and expenditures in recent decades are indicative of the rapid growth taking place at these levels of government, and there has been similar growth at the municipal level as well.

Analysis of federal revenue shows dependence prior to the First World War almost entirely on customs and excise. The war required large increases in these and finally in 1917 the introduction of an income tax. This, and sales taxes begun in 1920, soon became of paramount importance. Expenditures similarly underwent remarkable changes with welfare and defence charges assuming larger proportions and interest on the national debt seeming of less significance than in earlier decades. Included among the 'other' expenditures of the federal government are increasingly substantial payments to the provinces.

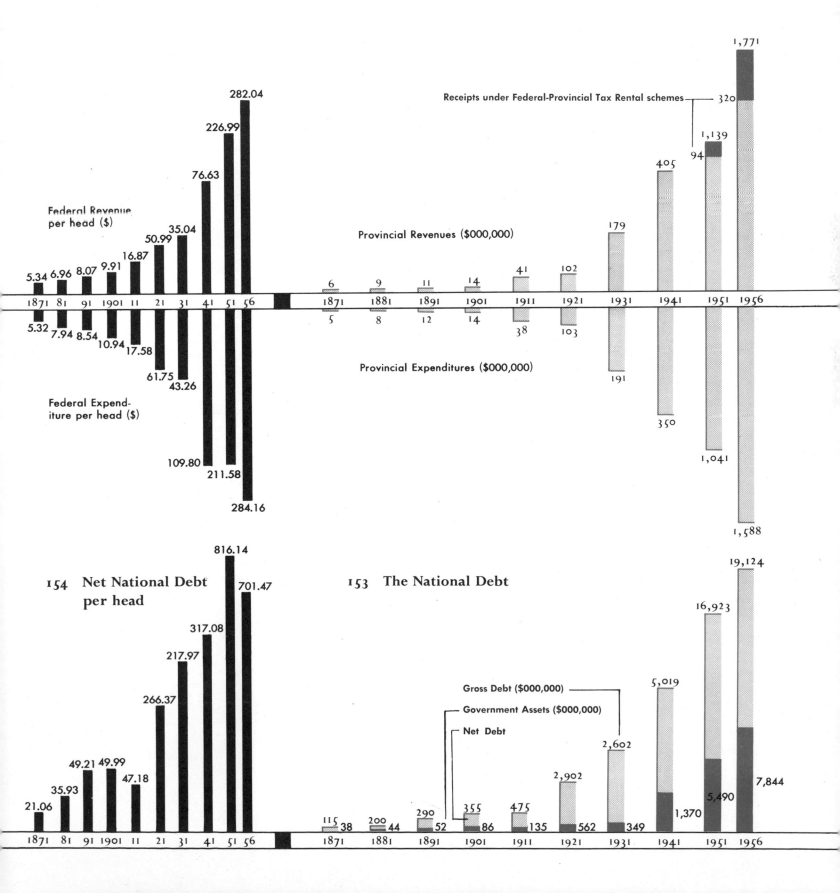

151 Federal Revenue and Expenditure per head

152 Total Provincial Revenues and Expenditures

Federal Revenue per head ($)

282.04
226.99
76.63
50.99
35.04
16.87
9.91
8.07
6.96
5.34

1871 81 91 1901 11 21 31 41 51 56

5.32
7.94 8.54
10.94
17.58
61.75
43.26
109.80
211.58
284.16

Federal Expenditure per head ($)

Receipts under Federal-Provincial Tax Rental schemes — 320 94

1,771
1,139
405
179
102
41
14
11
9
6

1871 1881 1891 1901 1911 1921 1931 1941 1951 1956

5
8
12
14
38
103
191
350
1,041
1,588

Provincial Revenues ($000,000)

Provincial Expenditures ($000,000)

154 Net National Debt per head

816.14
701.47
317.08
217.97
266.37
49.21 49.99
47.18
35.93
21.06

1871 81 91 1901 11 21 31 41 51 56

153 The National Debt

Gross Debt ($000,000)

Government Assets ($000,000)

Net Debt

19,124
16,923
5,019
2,602
2,902
475
355
290
200
115

38
44
52
86
135
562
349
1,370
5,490
7,844

1871 1881 1891 1901 1911 1921 1931 1941 1951 1956

SELECTED BIBLIOGRAPHY

In addition to works listed below the following periodicals contain valuable articles: *The Beaver, The Canadian Geographical Journal, The Canadian Historical Association's Annual Report,* the *Canadian Historical Review,* and the *Canadian Journal of Economics and Political Science.*

General Works

Birch, J. W.
Maps Topographical and Statistical
Oxford, 1949
Brebner, J. B.
North Atlantic Triangle   New Haven, 1945
Burpee, L. J.
An Historical Atlas of Canada
Toronto, 1927
Canada:
Department of Mines and Technical Surveys, Geographical Branch
Atlas of Canada   Ottawa, 1957
Dominion Bureau of Statistics
Canada Year Books   Ottawa, 1905–
Censuses of Canada, 1871, 1881, 1891, 1901, 1911, 1921, 1931, 1941, 1951   Ottawa
Public Archives
Catalogue of Maps, Plans and Charts in the Map Room of the Dominion Archives, compiled by H. R. Holmden
Ottawa, 1912
Creighton, D. G.
Dominion of the North   2nd ed.
Toronto, 1957
Currie, A. W.
Economic Geography of Canada
Toronto, 1945
Easterbrook, W. T. and H. G. J. Aitken
Canadian Economic History   Toronto, 1956
Glazebrook, G. P. de T.
History of Transportation in Canada
New Haven, 1938
Graham, G. S.
Empire of the North Atlantic: the Maritime Struggle for North America
Toronto, 1950
Hutchison, B.
The Struggle for the Border   Toronto, 1955
Kennedy, W. P. M.
Statutes, Treaties and Documents of the Canadian Constitution   Toronto, 1930
Laval, Université de, Institut d'Histoire et de Géographie
Collection de cartes anciennes et modernes pour servir à l'étude de l'Histoire de l'Amérique et du Canada. Préface par Marcel Trudel   Quebec, 1948
Lower, A. R. M.
Colony to Nation   2nd ed.   Toronto, 1957
Mackintosh, W. A. and W. L. G. Joerg, eds.
Canadian Frontiers of Settlement   9 vols.
Toronto, 1934–38
McInnis, E.
The Unguarded Frontier, A History of American-Canadian Relations
New York, 1942
Paullin, C. O.
Atlas of the Historical Geography of the United States   Washington, 1932
Pratt, J. W.
A History of United States Foreign Policy
New York, 1958

Prowse, D. W.
A History of Newfoundland from the English, Colonial and Foreign Records
London, 1895
Putnam, D. F.
Canadian Regions: A Geography of Canada
London, 1952
Robbins, J. E., ed.
Encyclopedia Canadiana   Ottawa, 1957–8
Rose, J. H., A. P. Newton, and E. A. Benians, general eds.
Cambridge History of the British Empire VI, Canada and Newfoundland
Cambridge, 1930
Shortt, A. and A. G. Doughty, eds.
Canada and its Provinces   23 vols.
Toronto, 1913–17
Shotwell, J. T., ed.
The Relations of Canada and the United States   25 vols.
New Haven and Toronto, 1936–45
Stanley, G. F. G.
Canada's Soldiers, 1604–1954: The Military History of an Unmilitary People
Toronto, 1954
Taylor, G.
Canada: A Study of Cool, Continental Environments and their Effect on British and French Settlement   London, 1947
Wade, M.
The French Canadians, 1760–1945
Toronto, 1955

Exploration and Development to 1763

Biggar, H. P.
The Precursors of Jacques Cartier, 1497–1534: A Collection of Documents Relating to the Early History of the Dominion of Canada   Ottawa, 1911
The Works of Samuel de Champlain (Champlain Society)   6 vols.
Toronto, 1922–36
The Voyages of Jacques Cartier: published from the originals with translations, notes and appendices   Ottawa, 1924
Brebner, J. B.
New England's Outpost: Acadia before the Conquest of Canada   New York, 1927
The Explorers of North America, 1492–1806   Anchor Book ed.
Garden City, 1955
Brouillette, B.
La Pénétration du Continent Américain par les Canadiens Français   Montreal, 1939
Burpee, L. J., ed.
Journals and Letters of Pierre Gaultier de Varennes de la Vérendrye and his Sons (Champlain Society)   Toronto, 1927
The Search for the Western Sea   2 vols.
Toronto, 1935
The Discovery of Canada   Toronto, 1944
Burt, A. L.
The Old Province of Quebec   Toronto, 1933
Canada:
Public Archives
Sixteenth Century Maps Relating to Canada: a check-list and bibliography
Ottawa, 1956

Christy, M., ed.
The Voyages of Captain Luke Fox of Hull and of Captain Thomas James of Bristol in Search of a North-West Passage in 1631–1632   (Hakluyt Society)
London, 1894
Crouse, N. M.
La Vérendrye, Fur Trader and Explorer
Toronto, 1956
Doughty, A. G. and C. Martin, eds.
The Kelsey Papers   Ottawa, 1929
and D. A. McArthur, eds.
Documents Relating to the Constitutional History of Canada, 1791–1818
Ottawa, 1914
and N. Story, eds.
Documents Relating to the Constitutional History of Canada, 1819–1828
Ottawa, 1935
Ganong, W. F.
'The Cartography of the Gulf of Saint Lawrence from Cartier to Champlain', *Transactions of the Royal Society of Canada, section II*   Ottawa, 1889
Harrisse, H.
The Discovery of North America. A Critical Documentary, and Historic Investigation, with an Essay on the Cartography of the New World   London, 1892
Innis, H. A.
The Fur Trade in Canada   2nd ed.
Toronto, 1956
Jenness, D.
The Indians of Canada   3rd ed.
Ottawa, 1955
Long, M. H.
History of the Canadian People   Vol. I, *New France*   Toronto, 1942
MacLennan, J. S.
Louisbourg from its Foundation to its Fall, 1713–1758   London, 1918
Munro, W. B.
The Seigniorial System in Canada
New York, 1927
Documents Relating to Seigniorial Tenure in Canada, 1598–1854   Toronto, 1908
Newton, A. P.
The Great Age of Discovery   London, 1932
Shortt, A. and A. G. Doughty
Documents Relating to the Constitutional History of the Canadian People   Vol. I
Ottawa, 1918
Stacey, C. P.
Quebec, 1759   Toronto, 1959
Stefansson, V., ed.
The Three Voyages of Martin Frobisher 2 vols.   London, 1938
Taylor, E. G. R.
Tudor Geography, 1485–1583
London, 1930
Late Tudor and Early Stuart Geography, 1583–1650. A Sequel to Tudor Geography, 1485–1583   London, 1934
Voorhis, E.
Historic Forts and Trading Posts of the French Regime and of the English Fur Trading Companies   Typescript
Ottawa, 1930
Wagner, H. R.
The Cartography of the North West Coast of America to the Year 1800   2 vols.
Berkeley, 1937
Williamson, J. A.
A Short History of British Expansion 4th ed.   London, 1953

Winsor, J.
Narrative and Critical History of America
Vols. II, III, IV
Boston and New York, 1889
Cartier to Frontenac. Geographical Discovery in the Interior of North America in its Historical Relations, 1534–1700
Boston and New York, 1894
Wrong, G. M.
The Rise and Fall of New France 2 vols.
Toronto, 1928

British North America, 1763–1867

Bemis, S. F.
Jay's Treaty: A Study in Diplomacy and Commerce New York, 1923
Campbell, M. W.
The North West Company Toronto, 1957
Cowan, H. I.
British Emigration to British North America, 1783–1837 Toronto, 1928
Creighton, D. G.
The Empire of the St. Lawrence
Toronto, 1956
Currie, A. W.
The Grand Trunk Railway of Canada
Toronto, 1957
Galbraith, J. S.
The Hudson's Bay Company as an Imperial Factor, 1821–1869 Toronto, 1957
Ganong, W. F.
'A Monograph of Historic Sites in the Province of New Brunswick', *Transactions of the Royal Society of Canada, section II*
Ottawa, 1899
'A Monograph of the Origins of Settlements in the Province of New Brunswick', *Transactions of the Royal Society of Canada, section II* Ottawa, 1904
Hansen, M. L. and J. B. Brebner
The Mingling of the Canadian and American Peoples New Haven, 1940
Hind, H. J.
Narrative of the Canadian Red River Exploring Expedition of 1857, and of the Assiniboine and Saskatchewan Exploring Expedition of 1858 2 vols.
London, 1860
Landon, F.
Western Ontario and the American Frontier
New Haven, 1941
Lower, A. R. M.
The North American Assault on the Canadian Forest New Haven, 1936
Macdonald, N.
Canada, 1763–1841. Immigration and Settlement. The Administration of Imperial Land Regulations London, 1929
Mackenzie, A.
Voyages from Montreal, on the River St. Lawrence, through the Continent of North America, to the Frozen and Pacific Oceans; in the years 1789 and 1793
London, 1801
Martin, C.
Lord Selkirk's Work in Canada
Oxford, 1916
Morton, A. S.
History of the Canadian West to 1870–71
London, n.d.
Morton, W. L.
Manitoba, A History Toronto, 1957
Nicholson, N. L.
The Boundaries of Canada, its Provinces and Territories Ottawa, 1954
Ormsby, Margaret A.
British Columbia: A History
Toronto, 1958

Paterson, G. C.
Land Settlement in Upper Canada
Toronto, 1921
Rich, E. E.
The History of the Hudson's Bay Company 1670–1870: Vol. I, 1670–1763
London, 1958
Shippee, L. B.
Canadian-American Relations, 1847–1874
New Haven, 1935
Stacey, C. P.
Canada and the British Army, 1846–1871
New York, 1938
Tucker, G. N.
The Canadian Commercial Revolution, 1845–1851 New Haven, 1936
Tyrrell, J. B., ed.
David Thompson's Narrative of his Explorations in Western America 1784–1812
Toronto, 1916
United Kingdom
The Journals, Detailed Reports, and Observations Relative to the Exploration by Captain Palliser, of that Portion of British North America . . . between the Western Shore of Lake Superior and the Pacific Ocean during the Years 1857, 1858, 1859, and 1860 London, 1863
Vancouver, J., ed.
A Voyage of Discovery to the North Pacific Ocean . . . under the Command of Captain George Vancouver 3 vols.
London, 1798
Wood, W., ed.
Select British Documents of the Canadian War of 1812 (Champlain Society) 3 vols.
Toronto, 1920
Wright, E. C.
The Loyalists of New Brunswick
Ottawa, 1955

Founding a Nation, 1867–1914

Canada:
Department of Mines and Technical Surveys, Geographical Branch
An Introduction to the Geography of the Canadian Arctic. Canadian Geography Information Series No. 2 Ottawa, 1951
Hedges, J. B.
Building the Canadian West; The Land and Colonization Policies of the Canadian Pacific Railway New York, 1939
Innis, H. A. and A. R. M. Lower
Settlement of the Forest and Mining Frontiers Toronto, 1936
Mackintosh, W. A.
Prairie Settlement: The Geographic Setting
Toronto, 1934
Macoun, J.
Manitoba and the Great North-West
Guelph, 1882
Morton, A. S. and C. Martin
History of Prairie Settlement and Dominion Lands Policy Toronto, 1938
Stanley, G. F. G.
The Birth of Western Canada
London, 1936
Tansill, C. C.
Canadian-American Relations, 1875–1911
New Haven, 1943
Taylor, A.
Geographical Discovery and Exploration in the Queen Elizabeth Islands
Ottawa, 1955
Wright, J. F. C.
Saskatchewan, the History of a Province
Toronto, 1955

Wars and Expansion since 1914

Brown, F., ed.
The War in Maps: An Atlas of the New York Times Maps New York, 1946
Dunbar, M. and K. R. Greenaway
Arctic Canada from the Air Ottawa, 1956
Glazebrook, G. P. de T.
A History of Canadian External Relations
Toronto, 1950
Mackay, R. A., ed.
Newfoundland: Economic, Diplomatic, and Strategic Studies Toronto, 1946
Nicholson, G. W. L.
Official History of the Canadian Army in the Second World War. II, The Canadians in Italy, 1943–1945 Ottawa, 1957
Schull, Joseph
The Far Distant Ships. An Official Account of Canadian Naval Operations in the Second World War Ottawa, 1952
Stacey, C. P.
The Canadian Army, 1939–1945
Ottawa, 1948
An Official History of the Canadian Army in the Second World War. I, Six Years of War: the Army in Canada, Britain and the Pacific. III, The Victory Campaign, The Operations in North-West Europe, 1944–1945 Ottawa, 1955, 1960
Tucker, G. N.
The Naval Service of Canada: Its Official History. I, Origins and Early Years. II, Activities on Shore during the Second World War Ottawa, 1952

Main Economic and Political Trends since 1867

Canada:
Report of the Royal Commission on Dominion-Provincial Relations. Book I: *Canada, 1867–1939* (Rowell-Sirois Report)
Ottawa, 1940
Dominion Bureau of Statistics
Canadian Mining Statistics, 1886–1956; Mining Events, 1604–1956 Ottawa, 1957
National Accounts, Income and Expenditure, 1926–1950 Ottawa, 1951
Prices and Price Indexes, 1949–1952
Ottawa, 1954
Revised Index of Industrial Production, 1935–1957 Ottawa, 1959
Secretary of State of Canada
Organization of Government of Canada
Ottawa, 1958
Chapman, J. D. and D. B. Turner, eds.
British Columbia Atlas of Resources
Vancouver, 1956
Firestone, O. J.
Canada's Economic Development, 1867–1953 London, 1958
McIvor, R. C.
Canadian Monetary, Banking and Fiscal Development Toronto, 1959
Taylor, K. W., ed.
Statistical Contributions to Canadian Economic History Toronto, 1931
Underhill, F. H., ed.
The Canadian Northwest: Its Potentialities
Toronto, 1959

INDEX

Page references in roman type are to the maps ; *in italic, to the text.*

Printed in Great Britain by
Thomas Nelson and Sons Ltd, Edinburgh